I0875924

How to Direct a

Concert

This is the first comprehensive, professional manual on concert direction, providing step-by-step guidance on transforming live music performances into intentional theatrical experiences through set design, lighting, blocking, audience engagement, and emotional continuity.

While theater and film have established norms and training for directors, concerts have lacked an equivalent discipline—leaving a creative leadership void in most productions. This book argues that concert direction is not only a missing link but an emerging profession whose time has come, just as it did in the evolution of modern theater. Drawing from decades of field-tested experience, *How to Direct a Concert: A Guide to Stage Direction and Design for Rock, Pop, Hip Hop, EDM, and More* explains the unique position of a concert director and why the role is essential for creating memorable performances, as well as teaching readers how to craft emotionally resonant and visually compelling live shows for any musical genre. This accessible guide provides structure and strategy where none currently exist, offering practical tools to navigate the process of creating unforgettable live music experiences. Through case studies, readers gain both strategic frameworks and concrete techniques for transforming fragmented performances into intentional, memorable shows that elevate the artist's stature and redefine what modern live music can be.

This book is written for performing artists, artist and tour managers, concert producers and promoters, students in live event production and performing arts programs, and industry professionals looking to elevate the quality of live music experiences.

Sam Pocker is a contemporary artist who also works in video, music, and performance. His work has been featured in *The Wall Street Journal, NPR Morning Edition, The Los Angeles Times, The New York Daily News, WPIX 11 News at Ten*, and many other media outlets.

How to Direct a Concert

A Guide to Stage Direction and Design for Rock, Pop, Hip Hop, EDM, and More

Sam Pocker

Routledge
Taylor & Francis Group
NEW YORK AND LONDON

Designed cover image: © Sam Pocker

First published 2027
by Routledge
605 Third Avenue, New York, NY 10158

and by Routledge
4 Park Square, Milton Park, Abingdon, Oxon, OX14 4RN

Routledge is an imprint of the Taylor & Francis Group, an informa business

Library of Congress Cataloging-in-Publication Data
Names: Pocker, Sam author
Title: How to direct a concert : a guide to stage direction and design for rock, pop, hip hop, EDM, and more / Sam Pocker.
Description: New York, NY : Routledge, 2027. | Includes index.
Identifiers: LCCN 2026016173 (print) | LCCN 2026016174 (ebook) | ISBN 9781041154198 hardback | ISBN 9781041154174 paperback | ISBN 9781003679332 ebook
Subjects: LCSH: Concerts--Production and direction | Popular music--Production and direction | Rock concerts--Stage-setting and scenery
Classification: LCC ML3790 .P58 2027 (print) | LCC ML3790 (ebook) | DDC 780.78--dc23/eng/20260709
LC record available at https://lccn.loc.gov/2026016173
LC ebook record available at https://lccn.loc.gov/2026016174

ISBN: 978-1-041-15419-8 (hbk)
ISBN: 978-1-041-15417-4 (pbk)
ISBN: 978-1-003-67933-2 (ebk)

DOI: 10.4324/9781003679332

Typeset in Helvetica
by KnowledgeWorks Global Ltd.

Contents

Foreword

Where has this book been all my life? Even from my earliest concert experiences, and especially since I started performing in my teen years during the opening salvos of punk rock, I've always wondered what makes some artists' performances stand apart from the pack. As a music professional for all of my adult life, I've never stopped wanting to learn how to improve my own concert productions, elevate the audience's experience, heighten their expectations, and deliver the goods. But until now, a book that explained, with authority, how to do it … just did not exist.

The first rock spectacle I ever attended was David Bowie's epic *Diamond Dogs* tour. It was in Tampa, Florida, and the show nearly didn't happen when a semi truck carrying the massive sets crashed into a Florida swamp—the result of a bee sting to the driver. Bowie, in the best show-must-go-on tradition, carried on and still delivered a brilliant, theatrical performance with minimal props, thanks to the intense planning and staging already in place. Soon after, Alice Cooper's *Welcome To My Nightmare* tour rolled through town. Each song was directed as a theatrical vignette by director David Winters, like a scene in a movie or play. Again, I was blown away by the precision, presence, and confidence. Even as an audience member, it was clear in both cases that these indelible moments did not happen by accident, luck, or even the power of personality. They had all been carefully planned and practiced. While entertaining thousands, these kinds of moments create superstars.

Concerts of this caliber are crafted with intention and theatrical intelligence by a team of professionals working toward a common goal. This book outlines, step by step, how a network of people and a formidable web of details can be harnessed—from lights-up to the final encore and beyond.

Artists, myself included, can be resistant to direction. It's a natural reflex for some, a result of psychology, ego, force of habit, and just plain stubbornness. But look at the artists whose concerts have made history. Even with the kind of strong will and self-assurance that is the stuff of legend, they were all dedicated to their craft and careers enough to know they needed help to realize their vision. Without direction and discipline, it would have been impossible to do what they did, not least of which was raising the bar for the art and commerce of the entire concert industry.

The book you now hold in your hands is exactly that: a *handbook* for concert planning and direction. It's a helpful checklist and so much more. It is an instigator. It is an inspiration. It gets into your head and changes the way you think about concert production. With striking clarity, it helps you see musicians, choreographers, lighting, sound, set and costume designers, and technicians as part of a multi-armed creative team, and that each member must be fully on the same page.

In the 2010s, I taught a course called Stage Presence at the Clive Davis Institute of Recorded Music at New York University. If this book had existed then, I would have made it a required reading for my students. Although the author has written it with directors in mind, it can be an invaluable tool for the other half of the equation: the performing artists themselves. By recognizing the director's role and reasoning, they can be more receptive and less resistant to direction. For artists who don't have the funds or clout to hire a director yet, this book can serve as a powerful starting point, help focus their intent and energy, and give them a tremendous head start that will serve them well when they can hire one.

Whether you are a director or performer, read this book and carry its wisdom with you every step of the way. The point, and the end goal, is to make your concert a great, lasting work, even though it exists only during those brief hours and minutes on the stage. The impact made on a concert stage can reverberate over time. Over years ... decades. It can make or break careers. Let's make it great.

Richard Barone
Musician, producer, and author
New York City

Books:
Frontman: Surviving the Rock Star Myth
Music + Revolution: Greenwich Village in the 1960s

Introduction

I sat down to write this book because, to the best of my knowledge, no one else has.

As of this writing, the concert industry is valued at approximately $172 billion annually, yet not one book has been written specifically on directing concerts. This absence alone highlights the challenge you're about to face.

In this book we will go step-by-step through every aspect of concert production that requires direction, including set design, lighting, sound design, blocking, choreography, dialogue, audience engagement, tailoring the show for different types of venues, bringing special guests into the production on a limited basis, and other similar concepts.

There are, of course, many excellent guides to directing theater. But directing a concert presents a unique set of challenges. Here are a few examples:

Unlike a play or musical, concerts rarely come with a script. There may be a setlist, storyboards, cue sheets, or style guides, but no script outlines the exact words and actions.

Whereas theater typically takes place in a consistent venue, concerts happen in venues of vastly different sizes and layouts, some without even a proscenium arch or seating.

Concerts also thrive on audience participation—a quality that might derail a play but enhances the experience of a live performance.

Additionally, concert production requires a practical focus on portability. Sets, lights, and even pyrotechnics are designed for ease of assembly, breakdown, and transportation, rather than for a permanent space where visual effects could be precisely tailored.

Moreover, a concert can succeed without a traditional narrative arc, plot points, or even dialogue. When concert dialogue appears, it's often simplistic, the epitome of which might be the timeless "Hello Cleveland!"

Concert rehearsals, too, can be shorter than those for plays or musicals, as performers often already know the music well.

Finally—and perhaps most significantly—is the role of the performer. In traditional theater, the performer acts out a role; in a concert, the artist embodies both the performer and the creative force behind the experience, often with minimal understanding of what contributes to a show's flow beyond their ability to engage an audience.

There are many instances of performers working simultaneously as the directors of their own tours. This is never a good idea. Even when a performer has a theatrical background, they are still relying on video playback to see how the show looks. A theatrical experience is different from a recorded version of it. You can always spot these tours because they look great on video, but in person the audience feels disengaged and one step removed from the show, as if they are attending a TV taping.

You might wonder what qualifies me to write this book. I've spent 30 years attending hundreds of concerts annually, talking to crew members and technicians, listening backstage, and learning everything I could about what makes a show work. In this process, I discovered that surprisingly few concert tours even have directors. Often, lighting or sound engineers fill this role by default.

Frustrated by the poor quality of so many shows and the apparent lack of awareness of artists of the importance of direction, I felt compelled to write this book. My hope is to pass along what I've learned to help future generations create better, more intentional performances.

In recent years, I have begun to create YouTube videos analyzing what works and what doesn't in concert footage. Despite my disclaimers, these videos received mostly negative feedback from die-hard fans who felt I was being overly critical. This is another challenge in concert directing: fanatics who resist any critique of their favorite artists. But I encourage you to see past this and focus on creating a truly memorable experience for the audience.

By choosing to read this book, you're taking on a responsibility: to elevate live shows beyond mere merchandise and drink sales and to present something new, original, honest, and inspiring to the public.

Chapter 1
Why Concerts Need Directors

Why Do Concerts Need a Director?

This is a reasonable question, especially when you consider that most touring shows go out on the road without one. A closer look at a touring crew reveals a striking composition: the majority of personnel are technicians, logistics managers, or operations experts—individuals trained in the mechanics of the show, not its artistic direction.

And yet, if you ask around a touring production who the director is, at least three people will raise their hands. The lighting designer, the tour manager, maybe even the lead artist themselves—all might claim ownership over the show's creative vision. But this confusion is exactly the point: in most concerts, there is no unified artistic authority guiding the experience from beginning to end. This absence leaves a vacuum that's usually filled by default, not by design.

Among the multiple people who may claim the title of "director" in a touring production, the musical director often holds the most weight. They are typically the closest to the artist, working directly with the band, arranging the setlist, refining transitions between songs, and managing the sound of the show. Their influence is real and often substantial.

But while the musical director might shape the sonic flow of the evening, they are not a stage director. Their focus is on what the show sounds like, not what it feels like visually, spatially, or emotionally.

They may ensure that the band hits every cue and that the arrangements are tight, but they are not trained to think about narrative arc, visual consistency, or audience immersion. In many cases, the musical

DOI: 10.4324/9781003679332-1

director ends up unintentionally occupying the directorial role simply because no one else is doing it—and that's part of the problem.

A concert needs both: someone to direct the music and someone to direct the show. Those are two different jobs, and when they're collapsed into one, something is always lost.

There are three basic mistakes that arise when concerts lack a dedicated director. First, the stage show becomes a patchwork of ideas based on what the artist personally thinks looks cool. But most artists—no matter how creatively gifted—do not have formal training in theatrical storytelling, spatial design, or audience psychology.

Occasionally, an artist with a strong theatrical background wants to direct their own show. This causes a reverse but equally difficult problem: they try to throw the kitchen sink into the production, and it ends up becoming meandering, self-indulgent, and expensive.

As a result, visuals may clash with each other, the pacing of the show can feel erratic, and moments that should feel profound instead fall flat. Without someone to shape the narrative and emotional arc of the show, it risks becoming little more than a playlist with light cues.

Second, artists often incorporate elements that, in their experience, reliably boost crowd engagement—call-and-response chants, pyrotechnics, sudden tempo drops, or crowd-surfing moments. While these may create spikes in energy, they're not always appropriate to the overall tone or message of the show. A truly effective concert director would contextualize these moments so they enhance, rather than disrupt, the experience. Not everything that "works" should be used; some things cheapen the integrity of the performance, or worse, alienate certain segments of the audience.

The third and perhaps most critical problem is that most concerts today are still staged as if it were the 1980s or 1990s. The structure, pacing, and expectations haven't evolved to match contemporary audiences. Meanwhile, ticket prices have skyrocketed, meaning that younger generations attend fewer concerts, have less experiential context, and often walk in with lowered expectations. In other words, today's shows are not only failing to push forward—they're also being consumed by audiences who no longer know what a great live experience can be.

A concert director, attuned to generational shifts and audience psychology, could radically redefine what a modern live show feels like.

The final and perhaps most overlooked obstacle is the audience itself. Many concertgoers today attend for reasons that have little to do with watching the show: to take selfies, to socialize, to post videos online.

A well-directed show doesn't just rely on spectacle; it knows how and when to focus the crowd, how to design the stage to guide their eyes, and how to build emotional and narrative tension.

The late architect Mark Fisher, who designed many of the world's most iconic stadium productions, understood this better than anyone. He once explained that the Rolling Stones opened their concerts with fireworks so American audiences would understand the show had started and where to look—and then ended with fireworks to signal the conclusion. These weren't just gimmicks; they were intentional directorial choices designed to shape audience behavior.

Misconceptions about Directing in Live Music

The most pervasive misconception about directing in concert production is that anyone trying to impose an artistic vision is "difficult" and ultimately makes the show harder to execute. This perception typically comes from within the technical crew—especially sound engineers, lighting designers, and stage managers—who are often the de facto leaders of the production. These shows are, in many ways, construction sites: massive logistical undertakings run by highly skilled professionals whose primary concern is stability, efficiency, and safety. But because the culture of touring production is so rooted in construction and mechanics, there's little space made for aesthetics.

Taste is often treated as a luxury—or worse, a threat. When a director enters the process and starts making creative decisions, it can disrupt the crew's routines and priorities. The response is often resistance, not collaboration.

After all, most people still think of a concert as just a band "rocking out" onstage while the audience "rocks out" below. In that framework, artistic direction seems unnecessary—something that gets in the way. But this mindset is exactly what keeps so many shows from evolving beyond chaos into craft.

Another widespread misconception is that a concert doesn't need structured direction because the artist will "fill in the gaps." The assumption is that if you provide a setlist and a few broad staging cues, the artist's charisma and experience will take care of the rest. In some cases, this improvisational approach is even encouraged—as if spontaneity is inherently more authentic or exciting. But while many artists are brilliant performers, most do not come from a theatrical background. They are not trained to shape a scene, control the pacing of a moment, or guide the emotional energy of a crowd over time.

One of the most common—and destructive—forms of improvisation occurs when artists speak between songs or even during songs, letting their real-world emotions override the emotional arc of the performance. Often, this happens because artists feel isolated from their fans and see the concert as their only chance to connect. As a result, they might launch into rambling monologues that have little to do with the tone or themes of the show. Even worse, they frequently interrupt musical breaks—carefully composed emotional moments—to shout things like, "What's up, (City Name)?" or "Is everybody having a good time?"

While these outbursts are meant to boost crowd energy, they actively undermine the music's emotional architecture. If a song is about control, heartbreak, or vulnerability, and the performer suddenly breaks character to pander to the crowd, the illusion is shattered. It's the theatrical equivalent of an actor breaking the fourth wall in the middle of a dramatic scene to ask the audience how their night is going.

The problem isn't just tone—it's believability. If the character singing about self-discipline and emotional strength suddenly veers into hypeman mode, the audience subconsciously stops trusting the performance. A director's job is to prevent these moments from derailing the show by creating intentional opportunities for connection—without sacrificing emotional continuity.

One of the most misleading assumptions is that "if the visuals are good, that's enough." In many modern shows, this belief manifests as a giant LED screen upstage playing unrelated or barely connected video content while the artist performs downstage. The assumption is that the screen will "fill the space" and keep the audience entertained visually—so much so that no further direction is necessary. But this creates a disjointed experience.

The audience sees one thing and hears another, and the disconnect becomes theatrical noise. It's not that visuals are bad—in fact, they can be incredibly powerful when used in service of the performance. But too often, they are tacked on as a kind of moving wallpaper, designed without consideration for the emotional tone, narrative arc, or physical choreography of the artist.

Sometimes the truth is harsher: there is no actual show at all—just a concert taking place in front of a digital billboard. This overreliance on projection not only reduces the potential for deep engagement but often makes the experience feel cold, distant, and emotionally flat. A director's role is not to balance the artist and the screen, but to question whether the screen should be there in the first place—and if it is, to ensure that it is meaningfully integrated into the overall storytelling.

A final and persistent misconception is that concerts are inherently too interactive or chaotic to be directed with the same precision as a legitimate theatrical production. The logic goes: theater is passive, concerts are interactive—and therefore, you can't expect the same level of environmental control. But this is a false binary. In reality, many concerts take place in legitimate theaters, and even those that don't still operate within fixed spaces, with controlled lighting, sound, and sightlines.

The difference isn't the venue—it's the expectation. Directors are often discouraged from trying to shape the audience's behavior, as if that were a lost cause in a concert setting. But directing is fundamentally about manipulating emotion and attention.

If you're doing your job well—crafting the pacing, staging, tone, and emotional flow of the show—then you can shape the audience's behavior. You can lead them into silence, into stillness, into awe.

You can create moments where they cheer, cry, or reflect. The audience will respond as they do in the theater—when the material earns it. The job of the concert director is not to fight the interactive nature of live music, but to use it strategically, so that the interactivity serves the show rather than distorting it.

Understanding the Audience's Expectations

At the core of every concert ticket purchase is a simple emotional transaction: someone hears a hit song, they feel something, and then they discover they can go see the person who made them feel that way. That's the hook. It's not really about the artist at first—it's about the feeling the song creates.

The listener thinks: "If the recorded version made me feel this way in my car, or in my headphones, or on the floor of my apartment … imagine how powerful it will be to feel that same thing live." That imagined amplification is the emotional anchor of most ticket sales. People don't just expect to hear the hit song—they expect to feel it more intensely than they ever have before. They're hoping for catharsis. They're expecting a memory. They've built a moment in their mind before they even enter the venue.

This is the emotional contract between artist and audience, whether it's acknowledged or not. And it places an enormous responsibility on the direction of the show. The "hit" can't just be thrown into the setlist like any other song. It has to be designed—framed, timed, and staged—to deliver on the weight of that expectation. If it comes too early, it feels cheap. If it comes too late, it feels manipulative. If it comes without any special attention, it feels dismissive. As a director, your job is not just to play the song—it's to deliver the feeling the audience came for, and ideally, to exceed it.

Of course, not every audience is coming for the hit song feeling. Artists who have been touring for decades attract a different kind of crowd, with a broader and more complex set of expectations. Some fans show up for nostalgia, some for tradition, some just to be in the same room as an icon.

The emotional stakes are different, and so is the performance contract. There are fans who want to hear the same banter they heard ten years ago, in the same voice, with the same lighting cues. For legacy artists, the show often becomes a kind of ritual—comforting in its familiarity. But this book is not primarily about those shows.

This book is for directors working with newer artists, or artists who are ready to evolve. If you're reading this, you're likely working with someone who isn't already set in their ways, who doesn't have 40 years of habits to protect.

You're working with someone who wants to build something intentional, innovative, and emotionally powerful from the ground up. That's why I'm focusing on this initial expectation—the idea that a concert is a place where someone goes to feel a specific feeling, more powerfully than they ever have before. Everything else builds from that starting point.

The second most prevalent type of audience member is not the diehard fan at all—it's the person who was brought along by someone else. They didn't buy the ticket, and they're not chasing the emotional high of a particular song. Statistically, this person might make up half the room, especially at early-career shows. They walk into the venue with little or no idea who the artist is, what kind of music they play, or what the show is about. Many of them are simply looking for a new environment in which to become intoxicated—legally or otherwise—among a large group of strangers.

A significant subset of this group may have even simpler motives: they came to meet someone, to hook up, to network, or to post something on social media that makes it look like they were part of a scene. This doesn't make them bad audience members, but it does make them unpredictable.

At least a quarter of the room, at any given show, may not even know why they're there—and may not be in a mental state to process the show with any level of focus. As a director, you have to account for that. You're not just directing for the fans—you're also directing for the people who are waiting to become fans. That means the first ten minutes of the show matter even more than you think. They don't just set the tone; they either pull people in—or lose them entirely.

With all of this in mind, it's worth addressing one of the most common hesitations people express when invited to a concert: "I don't know all the songs." It's such a frequent response that many fans stop inviting friends altogether unless they're already familiar with the artist. But this mindset reveals a deeper misunderstanding—not just about concerts, but about what a well-directed show can and should do.

A truly great show doesn't rely on familiarity. Someone should be able to walk in off the street, knowing nothing about the artist, having never heard a single track, and still feel completely engaged. The music might be in a different genre, a different style, even a different language—but if the show is directed well, it will still communicate. It will use visual storytelling, emotional pacing, rhythm, tone, and presence to reach the audience on a human level. That's the director's job: to make the experience legible, compelling, and alive for everyone, not just the people who showed up wearing merch.

This is where many shows fall short. They assume the room is full of fans, when in fact, a large portion of the audience is encountering the artist for the first time. Directing with that reality in mind doesn't dilute the experience for diehards—it strengthens it for everyone.

Chapter 2
How Concerts Differ from Legitimate Theater

No Script, No Fourth Wall

One of the clearest distinctions between theater and concerts is the presence—or absence—of a fourth wall. Most concerts don't have one. That's not a criticism; it's just the norm. Artists talk directly to the crowd, shout them out, gesture, banter, engage. The space between the performer and the audience is intentionally porous. But the lack of a fourth wall in live music doesn't mean that you can't have one—or that you shouldn't.

In fact, reintroducing the fourth wall into concert design is one of the most underused tools available to directors. Theatrical structure, when applied selectively, can unlock a new kind of intensity—one that draws the audience into the performance rather than merely inviting them to interact with it.

But if you're going to create a fourth wall—if you're going to construct a stage world in which the performer is not addressing the audience directly—there's one question you absolutely must answer: Who is the singer singing to? It sounds obvious, but you'd be surprised how many shows build out elaborate visuals and stage environments without ever resolving this basic problem.

Are they singing to their roommate? Their ex? The friend who ghosted them last year? Are they singing to their boss? Their mom? The delivery driver who shows up every Thursday with the same awkward smile? It doesn't matter who it is, as long as it's specific—and clear. The performer has to know who they're singing to, yes, but just as

DOI: 10.4324/9781003679332-2

importantly, the audience has to know, too. Before the first note hits, the crowd should already feel the shape of that relationship. Otherwise, they're left guessing, and the emotional weight of the song gets lost before it can land.

Think about how a Broadway musical works: each song is performed to someone, even if that someone isn't onstage. Sometimes it's a romantic partner, sometimes it's a rival, sometimes it's the singer themselves—but it's always clear. The audience isn't being performed at; they're eavesdropping. That's the magic of the fourth wall. It doesn't exclude the audience—it invites them into an imagined space where emotional truth can unfold without interruption.

This kind of intentionality changes everything. Every lighting cue, every movement, every line of sight becomes sharper—more intentional—because it's all oriented toward that invisible other. The audience may not see them, but they feel their presence in the way the performer carries the moment. Otherwise, you end up with something that looks theatrical but doesn't feel coherent. The visuals are moody, the lighting is dramatic, the band is tight—and yet, the audience doesn't know where to focus, or how to feel.

Take David Bowie's 1983 performance of "Cracked Actor" as an example. He sang the song holding up a skull—an unmistakable nod to *Hamlet*, where the protagonist famously monologues to the skull of Yorick. Bowie wasn't singing at the crowd. He was singing to the skull. That one decision turned what could've been a campy rock moment into a piece of theatrical provocation. The emotional force of the scene didn't come from lights or lasers. It came from the clarity of the dramatic relationship: man, skull, death.

This is what directors do. They help the artist find the frame. The song already exists. The performance already exists. What's missing is the dramatic container. And if you want to build a show that isn't just a sequence of disconnected songs, but a cohesive emotional experience, then you need that container—song by song, scene by scene.

There are dozens of theatrical devices you can borrow to make this work. The singer can write a letter. They can listen to a voicemail. They can sing to a projection, to a mirror, to a mask, to a locked door. They can sing to someone sitting silently on stage. They can sing while facing away, staring into a distant horizon. These are all ways of creating focus, tension, relationship. And every one of them is more compelling than just singing towards the balcony.

When you put the fourth wall in place, you're not cutting the audience out. You're inviting them to see something more intimate than if the artist were looking them in the eyes. You're creating a world—and letting them peek inside.

Another major difference between concerts and legitimate theater is emotional familiarity. In a concert, the audience already knows the lead. Or at least, they think they do.

This is not a neutral crowd walking in off the street. These are people with years of built-up feelings about the performer—memories, assumptions, projections. They've watched interviews. They've read rumors. They've posted lyrics as captions. They've cried in their cars to a song that felt like it was written just for them. And now they're standing in the same room as the person who soundtracked their breakup, their graduation, their worst summer, their best night.

That doesn't happen in traditional theater. When you go see *Hamlet*, you don't walk in thinking you know the guy playing Hamlet. If you've seen the play before, you're watching to see how this version interprets the role. If you haven't, you're coming in clean, with no emotional debt to the cast. The actors get to build their relationships with the audience from scratch.

But in a concert, that relationship is already fully loaded before the show even starts. And that changes the stakes.

It also introduces a unique tension: sometimes the audience is thrilled when their imagined version of the artist is confirmed—when the person onstage says or does something that aligns with what they've always believed. But sometimes they're disappointed, or even angry, when the illusion breaks. When the artist reveals a different side. When they speak in a new voice. When they change.

This preloaded emotional attachment isn't a bad thing—but it is a volatile one. It has to be handled with care. As a director, you can't treat the performer like a neutral character stepping onto a blank stage. You're not just building a show—you're managing a relationship the audience already believes they're in.

But ironically, one of the most powerful tools you do have is treating the performer like a blank slate—at least at first. To bring them in not as the version the audience expects, but as a character with no history yet, stepping into a new world. That strategy can buy you just enough space to reset the relationship. It asks the audience to put their projections on pause—just long enough to engage with what's actually happening on stage.

This is part of why artists like David Bowie and Madonna thrived on reinvention. With every tour, they changed the rules. New look, new sound, new context, new character. That constant evolution wasn't just a marketing choice—it was a way of shaking off the emotional residue from previous albums, previous versions, previous expectations. It made the audience watch more carefully, listen more closely. It reminded them that this wasn't just their version of the artist anymore—this was someone new, someone unpredictable, someone worth paying attention to.

Variable Venues and Technical Constraints

Another key difference—and one that's impossible to ignore when directing a concert—is the technical reality of touring. Unlike traditional theater, where you can count on a fixed environment, concert shows are nomadic. They have to function in wildly inconsistent spaces, night after night.

In theater, you know what you're working with. A proscenium arch. Wings on both sides. A fly system. Controlled lighting. A consistent backstage layout. Sightlines that were designed for drama, not drinks. But on tour? None of that is guaranteed.

And this variability isn't just aesthetic—it changes everything. The pacing of the show. The timing of entrances. The visibility of effects. Even the performer's energy can shift based on how the room holds sound or reflects light. A cue that landed perfectly in one venue might fall completely flat in another because the geometry is different.

This is the unglamorous but essential part of concert direction: you're not just crafting a show, you're engineering a portable experience. Something that can bend without breaking. Something flexible enough to survive bad weather, cramped stages, bad lighting angles, missing gear, or last-minute substitutions—without the emotional integrity of the show falling apart.

One of the most important and underrated variables from night to night is the height of the stage and the distance between the performer and the front row. That physical relationship shapes the entire emotional temperature of the show. If the artist is five feet above the crowd and separated by a barricade, it's a power position—more like an icon on a pedestal. If they're at eye level, a foot away from outstretched hands, it's intimate—almost confrontational. Same performer, same setlist, but the dynamic is completely different.

This is why, if you're directing a tour, you're not actually making one show. You're making three, maybe four, possibly five different versions of the same show—each tailored to a different type of venue, a different audience configuration, or a different night of the week. You're not just building for spaces. You're building for repeat customers, too. If you're playing the same city for multiple nights—and especially if you're an artist with hardcore fans—you can't just run the same exact show twice and expect the crowd to react the same way.

You also need to have one version of the show that drops the fourth wall entirely. This is your fallback. Your contingency plan. Your "just-in-case" version for when the gear doesn't make it, or the venue changes at the last minute, or the artist ends up doing a stripped-down promo event in a non-traditional space. No set, no props, no wings—just the performer and the audience. And far from being a compromise, this version can actually become one of the most powerful tools in your arsenal. Because when it's rare—when most of the tour maintains the fourth wall—those unexpected, unguarded shows where the artist connects directly with the audience feel special. Fans who are following the tour closely recognize that something different is happening, and that makes them feel even more connected. More inside the experience. And it reinforces that this artist knows how to show up under any circumstances—and still make it meaningful.

A smart tour design plans for this. You build a big show—something scalable—and then you strip it down as needed. That way, if the artist blows up mid-tour and suddenly jumps from 500-cap rooms to 5,000-seat theaters, the show can grow with them. You've already built the bones. You're not scrambling to retrofit a spectacle into a setlist that wasn't designed for it.

But to make that work, you have to be strategic. You don't just "wing it" when you see the venue. You need to know—well in advance—what kind of space you're walking into and which version of the show you're running. That means the team rehearses every version. It means you have lighting cues, blocking, prop placement, and stage entries mapped out for the wide room, the narrow room, the high stage, the no-stage, the full-rig, the stripped-down version. It means your artist knows how to switch between formats, and your crew isn't getting ambushed by last-minute surprises.

You don't want a tiny, minimal show playing in a cavernous venue—it'll feel empty, lost, underwhelming. But you also don't want a massive, overproduced show crammed into a low-ceiling bar where half the gear can't even be used. Both situations are avoidable if you build with flexibility in mind and treat every version of the show as equally real, equally rehearsed, and equally important.

And yet, 99 percent of the time, a concert tour still hits the road with barely more than a setlist. This is why you hear those cringe-inducing interviews with crew members and stagehands describing touring as "total chaos." They talk about how no two nights are the same, how things constantly go wrong, how they're making it up as they go. They wear the unpredictability like a badge of honor—as if the mess proves that they're doing something bold or authentic.

But that mindset should've died decades ago.

This isn't the Grateful Dead in the 1970s, with everyone high and half-lost in a haze of improvisation. This isn't a bandwagon of stoned geniuses feeling their way toward magic. That era is over. We are talking about professional productions, in professional venues, generating professional-level revenue. This is serious business—and it deserves to be treated with the same rigor and discipline as any legitimate theatrical enterprise.

The chaos is not a creative choice. It's just laziness disguised as freedom. It's dysfunction being passed off as authenticity. And more often than not, it's fueled by people who thrive on disorganization—who need the adrenaline of disaster to feel like they're doing something important.

But if you're serious about creating a transformative live experience—if you're serious about putting on a show that means something to people—then that kind of behavior has no place in your process. The audience didn't pay to see how well your crew can put out fires. They came to be immersed in something powerful, emotional, and unforgettable.

Real artists don't rely on chaos. They build the structure that allows for brilliance. They do the hard work so the moment can feel effortless.

The Myth of "Let The Music Speak for Itself"

There's a persistent myth in live music: the idea that the music should just "speak for itself."

You hear this a lot from songwriters, bands, and technically skilled performers who have spent years honing their craft. And what they're really saying, underneath that phrase, is usually one of two things: either they don't have any energy left to think about staging, or they don't know how to put on a show—and they're hoping no one will notice.

Sometimes it's dressed up as humility. Sometimes it's dressed up as artistic purity. But in practice, it's almost always a defense mechanism. It's a way of avoiding the reality that performing music live is not the same thing as putting on a show.

And if you're selling tickets, and people are coming into a room expecting an experience, then you owe them more than just a live version of the record. They came for something bigger than what they could get on headphones. They came for a show.

Now, to be fair, many artists genuinely don't know what that means. They haven't seen a lot of great shows. And the reason they haven't seen a lot of great shows is because they've spent all their time learning how to make music. That's not a character flaw—that's just a gap. And your job, as the director, is to fill it.

You've seen the shows. You've studied the arcs. You know how a well-staged moment can transform the room. Your job isn't to "fix" the artist. Your job is to take the brilliance that's already there and frame it—to translate it into a full performance that has shape, timing, rhythm, energy, and flow. You're not replacing the music. You're making it visible.

Another part of the challenge is the audience itself. As we discussed earlier, a good portion of the crowd doesn't know what to expect either. For some of them, just being in the same room as the performer is enough. The lights come down, the artist walks out, and they lose their minds. And that level of adoration can create a dangerous illusion for the artist: that standing onstage and playing the songs is all that's required.

But when the performance has no structure—when there's no pacing, no staging, no emotional arc—those same audience members will eventually start shouting at the stage, trying to insert themselves into the show. It's not because they're rude. It's because the show hasn't given them anything to hold onto.

And that's what we're trying to avoid. We don't want hype-driven chaos. We want engagement. We want atmosphere.

When you build a real show around the artist's music—when you elevate the material through design, intention, and direction—it changes how people see the artist. It makes them seem smarter, deeper, more thoughtful. It raises their stature without changing a single lyric or note.

If the artist lets you do your job, it's going to make them look better, but they have to be willing to collaborate. They have to understand that this isn't about ego, and it's definitely not about idol worship. In fact, one of the most dangerous things a performer can do is encourage blind adoration. Because once the audience sees you as a god, they'll eventually turn on you for not being divine.

What we're doing here is building something honest, exciting, and transformative. A piece of live art that's meant to move people, entertain them, shake them loose from their day. We are not here to replicate the record. We're here to play—in the truest, most joyful sense of the word. Play as in experiment. Play as in imagine. Play as in build a world and invite people into it.

That's what makes a concert a show—not just a song played well, but a moment performed with purpose.

One of the simplest—and most overlooked—ways to signal to the audience that they are here to see a show, and not just hang out at a party, is this: hand them a program.

It doesn't have to be fancy. You don't need to pay Playbill. You don't need glossy pages or full-color printing. You can take a single sheet of paper, run it through a black-and-white copier, fold it in half, and you've got a program. That's it. That's all it takes.

You could be playing in a nightclub. A warehouse. A DIY space. It doesn't matter. The moment you hand someone a program when they walk in the door, something shifts in their mind. They are no longer just part of a crowd. They are an audience. This isn't just a gig—it's a production. They are here to experience something. And they know it before the lights even go down.

That's a fundamental difference between a party and a piece of theater. At a party, people wait for something to happen. At a show, they know when it starts, and they're ready. A program sets that expectation. Quietly. Subconsciously. Clearly.

It's one of the cheapest, most effective tools you have—and almost no one uses it. Which is exactly why you should.

And once they've got that program in hand, there's one more simple move that seals the deal: right before the show starts, make a quick announcement asking everyone to silence their phones. Not because it's polite—but because it reminds them they're in a theater. It cues the audience to shift their mindset from casual to intentional. From crowd to witness. From chaos to focus.

Chapter 3
The Role of the Director in a Concert

Artistic Vision vs. Logistical Constraints

If Chapter 2 was about what concerts aren't—how they diverge from traditional theater—then this chapter is about the realities you can't escape. It's about the hard edges you run up against when you try to turn a concert into a fully realized piece of theater. Because no matter how ambitious your vision is, no matter how refined your aesthetic, you are ultimately working in a medium where someone has to stand onstage and make music come out of a speaker. And that means gear. Lots of it.

Microphones. Amps. Pedalboards. Drum kits. Racks. Mixers. Stands. Monitors. Cables that snake across the floor like a pile of spilled intentions. These objects aren't suggestions—they're requirements. Without them, there is no show. But very few of them are designed with theatrical beauty in mind. They're built for function. For volume. For clarity. For survival. The aesthetic is "tool," not "object." Which means that every piece of equipment on stage is a potential threat to your visual world.

And none are more insidious—or more essential—than microphones. Let's talk about the four kinds of microphones that you will encounter most frequently in concert production.

Handheld Microphones

Let's return to the handheld mic, because its symbolism goes beyond utility. It's not just a tool—it's a symbol, and a loaded one at that. It's undeniably phallic. It looks like a penis. That's not projection; it's basic

DOI: 10.4324/9781003679332-3

visual language. And once you notice it, you can't unsee it. A hypermasculine performer belting into a handheld mic is basically deep-throating a symbol of his own dominance, which can read as aggressively performative—or accidentally comic. On the flip side, a softer or more androgynous performer gripping that same mic might suddenly look out of place, or overwhelmed by the object, like it's too big for the emotional frame they're operating in. None of this is inherently bad. But all of it is visible. The mic becomes a symbol the moment it is held by the performer. If you don't address that symbolism, it's going to start pulling focus. And once the audience is distracted by that image, they're no longer inside the song. They're watching a metaphor instead of experiencing a moment.

(**Note:** If your performer is going to use a handheld microphone, make sure they know how to hold it. Most performers, even professionals, have no idea how to use a handheld mic properly. They wave it around like a wand, forgetting it has a directional capsule designed for precision, not theatrics. The result? Muddy vocals, inconsistent volume, feedback, and—most importantly—a loss of emotional connection. Because if the audience can't hear the words clearly, they can't feel them. So, step one in any handheld mic situation is education.)

Headset Microphones

Then there's the headset mic—the go-to for dancers, pop idols, and fitness instructors. It gives the performer freedom. It removes the need to grip anything. But unless you're staging a scene where it makes sense for someone to have a piece of machinery wrapped around their ears and curving toward their mouth, it can pull the audience right out of the world. Imagine a scene set in a bedroom. Or a street. Or a rooftop at 2am. Why is this person wandering around with what looks like a Bluetooth headset from the early 2000s? Why is this kid in a hoodie whispering their heart into a piece of plastic taped to their cheek? The tech might be invisible to the performer—but it's not invisible to the audience. You can't just act like it's not there. Either justify it inside the world of the scene, or find a different solution. Because when the gear doesn't match the moment, the fiction collapses.

Vintage Microphones

Vintage microphones are seductive. They carry weight. History. Style. You put one on stage and suddenly the air feels thicker, the lighting looks warmer, the performance seems more intentional. No one in the audience is going to ignore it. It's not a neutral object. It's a statement. And if that statement isn't backed up by the emotional or narrative logic of the scene, it creates friction. Why is this contemporary performer, in jeans and a hoodie, in the middle of a modern emotional breakdown, crooning into a 1940s RCA ribbon mic like they're headlining a post-war USO tour? It doesn't track. And audiences will notice. They'll wonder: is this a flashback? A dream? Is the performer playing a role? Is this a tribute act? The mic itself starts to rewrite the narrative. And unless that's the point, you're just confusing people. Use vintage gear when the scene can carry the visual weight of it. Otherwise, you're dragging antique furniture into a modern apartment and pretending it's not weird.

Hidden Microphones

Now let's talk about hiding mics—because sometimes the most powerful tech is the tech you never see. If you want to maintain the integrity of the world you're building on stage, start asking this question: Where would the voice naturally come from in this moment? If the performer is in a bedroom, singing in front of the mirror, maybe they're holding a hairbrush—so wire the hairbrush. Make it the mic. Hide the transmitter in the costume. Route the wire invisibly. Maybe the performer's on the phone—run the vocals through the phone. Make the object real. When tech disappears into the story, the audience stops questioning. They stop calculating. They believe. That's the goal. And it's entirely possible with a little pre-planning and some clever engineering. Directors need to start thinking this way—not just about where the mic goes, but what the mic is. What does it mean? Where does it live? How does it serve the scene? Every mic is an opportunity to either break the illusion—or deepen it.

This logic doesn't stop with microphones. It applies to everything—keyboards, drums, amps, monitors, cables, risers, pedalboards, DI boxes, even water bottles and setlists. Every piece of equipment on stage is either part of the story or it's a distraction from it. You can't just throw a drum kit into the corner and hope the audience doesn't notice the cymbals glowing under the soft amber light of an emotional monologue. You can't build a beautifully immersive set—an apartment, a forest, a dream—and then let a stack of amplifiers sit there like they wandered in from a bar gig down the street. Either integrate the gear into the design—match it to the color palette, build scenic elements around it, use lighting to fold it into the emotional tone of the moment—or find a way to hide it entirely. Not just visually, but emotionally. You're not designing for a neutral stage. You're designing for a world. And that world breaks the moment the tools of the trade start looking like clutter instead of character.

The final—and often most brutal—collision between artistic vision and logistical constraint happens outside the stage itself. You can control your lighting, your design, your blocking. But what about the banner above the bar advertising $3 tequila shots? What about the glowing neon beer logo in the corner, or the flickering EXIT sign that throws red light across your carefully composed emotional climax? What about the rows of empty seats in a half-filled arena, or the massive loading dock door that's still cracked open behind the stage? These are not hypotheticals. They are constants.

If you're playing in nightclubs, converted arenas, a local fair, outdoor pavilions, or multi-purpose venues, there will always be environmental noise—visual, spatial, emotional. And while you can't always control it, you can prepare for it. Build a toolkit. Research every venue ahead of time—photos, videos, tech specs. Know what weird signage you'll be dealing with. Know what venues need masking. Have modular pieces: drop cloths, collapsible backdrops, standing flats.

Some directors block the show to only use two-thirds of the stage and place a false wall at the back to enclose the world. Others bring U-shaped curtain rigs to hide the wings—though those don't hold up well outdoors. The point is, you have to think beyond the stage. Because the audience isn't just watching what's in the spotlight. They're absorbing the whole space. And if that space feels more like a bar than a show, then you've lost them—no matter how good the music is.

Collaboration with Artist, Crew, and Management

Before you do any work—before you block a single moment or sketch a single design—you need to make absolutely sure that everyone is actually on board. That sounds obvious. It's not. Because a lot of people will say yes to your vision without understanding what they're agreeing to. Especially the artist. They'll nod. They'll get excited. They'll say, "Let's make it a real show this time." And then the moment you try to get the drummer to hold a beat for a lighting cue, or ask a guitarist to take three steps stage left during a solo, the pushback starts. Suddenly it's "too rigid." Suddenly it's "not rock and roll." Suddenly you're "killing the vibe." What you're running into is culture—specifically, the deeply ingrained belief that a concert is a party, not a performance. And unless you dismantle that belief before you begin, the entire structure will buckle the moment the rehearsal gets difficult. Someone in the band will get lazy. Someone will "forget" their mark. Someone will roll their eyes when you talk about tension or pacing. That's the trap. And once you're in it, it's almost impossible to climb out. So have the hard conversation early. Make the stakes clear. This isn't a jam session. It's a piece of theater. Everyone has to be willing to meet the moment.

When they tell you it feels fake, that it's "killing the vibe" or making things too stiff, you need to be ready with examples that dismantle the myth. Because the truth is, the most iconic, high-energy, unforgettable performers in music history were choreographed to the second. ACDC? Every movement onstage—planned. Watch an old video, the bass player and the rhythm guitarist are always parallel. That's blocking. Run-DMC? Always choreographed. Michael Jackson, Prince, Madonna? Not one second of their shows was left to chance.

It's easy now to find videos online of rehearsals for all of their biggest tours.

Fast-forward to today's biggest stars: Taylor Swift, Harry Styles, Lady Gaga, Katy Perry, Sabrina Carpenter, Justin Bieber, Charli XCX—every single moment is rehearsed and executed with surgical precision. And yet it all feels spontaneous, which is the point. That's what makes it art, not chaos.

And then there's the crew. Good people. Skilled people. People who keep the whole thing from falling apart. But they are not going to understand what you're doing. Not right away. Because your goals are not their goals. Their job is to make sure the gear works. That the lights turn on. That the PA doesn't melt down. They are thinking in terms of function, not feeling. So when you start talking about "emotional arcs" or "light cues that breathe," you may as well be speaking French. That's not a knock—it's just reality. So the trick is to find the right crew. Not necessarily the most experienced—but the most open. Younger people tend to be better for this. They haven't calcified into habits yet. They're more willing to try something different. What you want to avoid is the guy who thinks he's the show. The kind of lighting op who dances at the desk like he's a fifth band member. That guy might be fun to watch for about ten seconds, but he's not doing his job—because his ego is louder than the light. And once that starts pulling focus, you've lost control of your show. You need a crew who understand that subtlety is a skill. That what you're building is atmosphere, not chaos. Find those people. And treat them like collaborators, not just tech support.

Finally, you have to get management on your side. This is not optional. Because when the show gets weird—and it will get weird—some of the audience is going to leave confused, disappointed, maybe even angry. Why? Because they came expecting a party. They came to drink, scream, and "rock out." And if you give them a show instead—something quiet, tense, strange, theatrical—they might not know what to do with it. And who are they going to complain to? Not the artist. Not you. They're going to complain to the manager. Which means, from the manager's point of view, you are the problem. Not because the show was bad, but because it made the audience feel something unexpected. That's dangerous in their world. Because their world runs on money. On margins. On merch sales and VIP upgrades and drink minimums. If your work feels like it's threatening the bottom line—even if it isn't—they will shut it down. So your job is to make sure they understand the value of what you're building. That it's not anti-fun. That it's not anti-fan. That it's just a different kind of engagement. You need to get them aligned before you do a single thing. Otherwise, you're building a house on a fault line.

What Makes a Show Feel "Directed"?

So what actually makes a show feel directed?

Here's a simple way to tell: if you've never seen a video of the Jackson 5 performing live, stop reading right now and go find one. Doesn't matter which—any of their early television appearances will do. Watch the whole thing. Pay attention. You will see five kids, in matching outfits, moving in sync, hitting every step, turning on the same beat, looking at the same mark, lifting their arms, spinning, pausing—together. Every smile is placed. Every gesture lands. And yet, none of it feels forced. None of it feels fake. What you're watching is pure direction. And you can tell—instantly—that they didn't just walk out on stage and "feel it out." You can tell their father made them rehearse it a thousand times in their living room until they could do it in their sleep. You can tell it was built, piece by piece, moment by moment. And it works. Because it doesn't feel robotic—it feels alive. An outside party watched each second and corrected every last thing that needed correction.

Now go watch a recent performance by Lana Del Rey. Any one of them. She's not dancing. She's barely moving. But everything around her is. Dancers, musicians, lighting cues—all moving around her in ways that feel completely natural. And yet, you can see it's been directed. You can feel the planning. Nobody is guessing. Everyone on stage knows where they are. Knows why they're there. Knows what their character is in the emotional world of the song. A guitarist sits on the couch like he lives there. A dancer leans against a lamppost like she's waiting for something. Every element of the scene is rooted in intention. And that's what direction is: not just blocking for the sake of movement, but emotional coherence across every body on stage. It's staging that understands performance is not just for the lead. Everyone is performing. Everyone is in character. Even if that character is just "the bass player who's tired of pretending he's not heartbroken."

Now compare that to a performance by Imagine Dragons. Or Green Day. Or Weezer. And you'll see the difference immediately. These are great musicians. Tight bands. Every note has been practiced into the ground. But nothing on stage has been directed. The lighting is random. The blocking is guesswork. The energy is there—but it's unfocused. The singer runs upstage and jumps off a riser because they feel like it. The bassist spins in a circle just because they've got space. The guitarist wanders over to the drum riser and then … just kind of stands there. You're not watching a show. You're watching a collection of people who all practiced their instruments, then showed up and hoped that would be enough. It's not. Because rehearsal gets you precision—but direction gets you meaning. And if you want the audience to feel something deeper than "that was really loud," then you're going to have to build it that way.

Chapter 4
Setlists and Show Structure

Narrative Flow without a Plot

If Chapter 3 was about working within the physical limits of gear and environment, this chapter is about something harder to define but just as essential: narrative flow. Not story. Not plot. Flow. That thing your audience feels but can't quite name. That slow emotional arc that keeps them engaged without ever needing to ask what's happening. Because nothing is happening—at least not in the traditional sense. This isn't a musical. It's a concert. And the moment you try to cram a musical's narrative spine into a concert's body, you get something deeply weird and unsatisfying.

If you've ever seen a jukebox musical (i.e. *Jersey Boys, Mamma Mia!*) you know what I mean. These shows are essentially concerts wearing a Halloween costume of plot. The songs come first, and everything else is reverse-engineered to make those songs "make sense" in context. It rarely works. Characters walk onstage, announce a problem, burst into a hit single, and leave. It's theatrical karaoke. You're watching grown adults try to sell emotional transitions that were clearly driven by licensing rights, not character motivation. No one believes it. Everyone claps anyway. And then they forget it five minutes later.

This is the trap we're avoiding.

A concert doesn't need plot. But it does need shape. It needs to move. It needs to evolve. It needs to feel like it's going somewhere—even if it's not telling a story in the traditional sense. That's where narrative flow comes in. And the key to building that flow is deceptively simple: a vision board. For every song. No exceptions.

DOI: 10.4324/9781003679332-4

Think of the vision board as a mood map. A distillation of everything the audience should be feeling in the 3–5 minutes that song lives on stage. Not what the song says or what the lyrics mean. Not the feeling that the character who is singing is necessarily feeling. The mood board should focus on what the moment feels like to the audience. That's the shift.

Don't make a mood essay. Choose one word. Only one. That word goes at the top of the board, in bold, all caps. That word is your north star. Next to that word write down the key of the song and circle it. Never put two songs in the same key next to each other.

Everything else—images, color palettes, references, textures, lighting cues, props, choreography, staging—must serve that one word. If you can't sum up the feeling of the song in a single word, you don't understand the moment yet. And if you don't understand it, you can't build it.

Sometimes, the word will match the song's original intent. A sad ballad is simply sad. Easy. But sometimes you're subverting the song. You're bending it. You're deliberately creating emotional dissonance. Maybe you're staging a joyful breakup song with images of absolute ruin. Maybe you're dressing a tragic torch song in bubblegum visuals to provoke a laugh—or discomfort. That's valid. That's allowed. But you still need the word. The audience's word. What they should feel. Not what the lyrics say. Not what the band intended. What you're creating.

Because everything that happens on stage—movement, lighting, costume, props, staging, even the silence between tracks—is a tool in service of that word. And when you string those words together across an entire setlist, you begin to see an emotional shape emerge. Not a plot. But a progression. And progression is what keeps the audience inside the world. That's narrative flow.

There's only one word that should never appear on any vision board. One feeling that is never, under any circumstances, part of the plan. That word is "bored."

If the audience is bored, you've lost them. Not because your lights weren't perfect or your blocking wasn't tight, but because something in the flow broke down. Boredom is the audience's way of telling you, "I don't know where I am, and I don't care what happens next." And once they feel that way, they start noticing everything you wish they wouldn't: the flickering EXIT sign, the mic that didn't get turned off, the tech stumbling through a scene change, the guy in the third row coughing during a ballad. Boredom turns the theater into a room again. And the whole point of this work—the costumes, the staging, the vision boards, the emotional architecture—is to make them forget where they are.

So use any word you want. Weird ones. Harsh ones. Contradictory ones. Just never choose bored. That's not a mood. That's a death sentence.

As a director, the clearest metric for boredom isn't silence. It isn't lack of applause. It's phones. Specifically, how many lit-up screens you see in the audience that aren't filming—and honestly, even the ones that are. If someone is looking at their phone during the show, they're not inside the moment. They've checked out. You can argue that they're just texting a babysitter or checking the time, but that's not your problem. Your job is to create a world so compelling they forget they even have a phone. Every screen you see glowing in the dark is a little glowing indictment of the energy in the room. So when you watch your own show, don't just watch the stage. Watch the crowd. Count the phones. If they're reaching for their pockets, something's broken. Fix it.

Balancing Energy, Tempo, and Emotional Breaks

Let's be clear: emotional architecture comes before setlists. Before blocking. Before costumes. Before anything touches the stage. If you're not building the shape of the night on paper first—using nothing but your vision boards and that one-word emotional spine per song—you're not directing. You're decorating chaos.

So what are we actually building?

We're building balance. Specifically, balance between three things: audience energy, performer energy, and emotional arc. And if any one of those tips too far in the wrong direction, the show collapses. Not all at once. Not dramatically. It just goes soft. Flat. Unmemorable. Which is worse than bad.

Before you can even begin to map out that arc, you have to know what kind of show you're building. What is the theme? What's the container?

If this show is built around a new album, what's that album about? Is it a breakup album? A manifesto? A love letter to the past? A processing of grief? A celebration of healing? What's the emotional thesis? And if it's a retrospective—an artist revisiting old work in a new way, maybe acoustically or in a different style—what's the tone of that revisit? Is it nostalgic? Is it bitter? Is it fun? Is it angry? Is it a reclamation?

You need to build a separate mood board for this. Not a song-by-song breakdown—but one single board that answers a simple question: What is this show about? What's the feeling that should thread through every single moment, even when the mood shifts? What's the spine? Because that's the thing you're holding onto when the arc gets complicated. That's your north star when you're making brutal cuts or reshuffling the emotional order of the night.

Once you've got the container, then you can start asking: how much emotional weight can the audience carry before they need release? How many songs in a row can the artist perform before they need to breathe? Will this show be one act, two acts, or even three? Will there be an intermission? Will the encores be distinct and planned—or will they be part of the flow? Will there be an opening act? And if so, how are we integrating that into the larger experience? Are they setting the tone? Sharing the world? Or breaking it?

These questions aren't logistical. They're structural. They define the rhythm of the entire experience. Because concerts—real ones, the kind we're building here—aren't just a string of songs. They're a journey. And journeys have shape. They have pacing. They have emotional breaks, not just because the body needs them—but because the story does.

Let's start building that container by focusing on the audience.

You cannot—repeat, cannot—ask an audience to feel the same thing over and over and expect them to stay engaged. Even if they love that feeling. Even if that's what they came for. If every song hits the same emotional note, if every moment on stage asks for the same physical or psychological response, they will burn out. Or worse, they'll tune out.

This is especially brutal when the artist has a consistent sound. If you're working with a pop artist—and most pop artists, by design, are working a very specific musical lane—you're going to run into this wall fast. Three bouncy uptempos in a row, and the audience's feet hurt. Three broody ballads, and they're mentally checking out. The music starts to blend. The show starts to feel like one long song with occasional outfit changes. You lose contrast. You lose shape. You lose them.

So what do you do?

You cheat.

You stage the same-feeling songs in totally different ways. You introduce visual contrast. You manipulate tempo—not musical tempo, emotional tempo. You change lighting, perspective, use of space. You move the performer differently. You shift tone, color, intimacy, scale. You introduce silence. Stillness. Chaos. Anything to break the pattern. If the music won't give you the variation, you create it through direction.

Now let's talk about the ending.

No matter what emotional terrain your show travels—dark, painful, weird, nihilistic—it has to land on its most positive moment. Not the biggest moment. Not the most famous. The most hopeful. The most human. You're not looking for a perfect resolution. You're looking for a window. A breath. A final feeling that sends the audience out into the night thinking not "That was heavy," but "That meant something."

The last mood board should be your brightest. Not necessarily the most literal or the most upbeat—but the most open. You want people leaving the space lifted, not crushed. Even if they don't realize why.

And then—maybe most importantly—you have to think about the performer.

Because none of this works if they fall apart halfway through.

If your show is a sprint with no water breaks, no costume changes, no space to reset or breathe, it will die. Fast. That performer is your entire show. And if they're pushing past their limits—vocally, physically, emotionally—just to get through the night, the audience will feel it. The mask will slip. The performance will hollow out. And once it hollows, it doesn't come back.

So you have to design breaks. On purpose. Not as filler, not as accidents, not as tech scrambles you hide behind projections—but as moments. Build in transitions. Build in silence. Build in time to change clothes, change energy, change posture. Use your dancers. Use your band. Use the space. Use the pause. The show should breathe like a body. Inhale. Exhale. Hold. Release.

Never repeat the same transition twice in a row. Ever.

Let's say the singer finishes a song, runs offstage to change costumes, and while they're gone, a video plays overhead. Fine. Clean. Functional. Then they return, hit the next track, and the show rolls on. But if they leave again—and you play another video—suddenly the trick becomes visible. The audience spots the pattern. They realize what you're doing. And once they realize you're covering for a quick change, they're no longer inside the show. They're doing math.

How many more songs? How many more videos? Are they all going to be like this?

The moment they start thinking about the mechanics, you've already lost.

Your goal is invisibility. Not distraction. Not noise. Seamlessness. The audience should never consciously register that the singer has left—or returned. They should feel like the world simply shifted, and the next moment arrived. Like breathing. Like magic. Not like stage management.

So yes—if your show has 15 songs, and your artist needs a costume change after every single one, then you'd better have at least 20 distinct transitions built, rehearsed, and ready. Not just different-looking. Different-feeling. Videos. Monologues. Scenelets. Instrumentals. Lighting states. Crowd work. Set movement. Shadow play. Silence. Whatever. Just never the same thing twice. And never anything that feels like a cover-up.

Because you're not hiding absences. You're weaving presence.

And if the illusion holds, the audience stays inside the spell.

Build the flow before you touch the setlist itself.

Now it's time to make a map. This can be on paper, a whiteboard, a digital notepad—whatever works for your brain. Start by writing something like: "We have 15 songs to perform in three acts, one encore, and no intermission." That's your headline. That's your container.

Draw four big boxes—one for each act, and a fourth for the encore. Put a clear dividing line between Act III and the encore. Then figure out if you're going to have an intermission, and if so, where it falls. Usually, it's safest to place the intermission after Act II. Mark that with a line as well.

Now for each act, ask a question: What does the lead character (the singer) want—and where do they have to go to get it? Once you know that, you know where the story begins, at least physically.

Example: If the album is about a breakup, does the show start with the breakup itself? Or the lead-up? Where does that moment happen—at a coffee shop? In a bedroom? In the back of an Uber?

Another example: If the album is about partying and having a good time, where does the party begin? Is it while the singer's still at work, watching the clock? After the parents are asleep? On a FaceTime call? Figure it out. The more specific the setting, the easier it is to direct.

And try to answer practical questions, too. Are they indoors or outdoors? Standing or sitting? Alone or in a crowd? Intimate or public?

Here's a basic example of how this can look—a 15-song show built around the theme of "partying and having fun." No plot. But a clear emotional arc.

Act I

Song 1: Late afternoon (5pm), restaurant job. Singer is getting ready to go home.

Song 2: Early evening (7pm), bedroom. Showering, changing clothes.

Song 3: Evening (9pm), outside club. Waiting in line.

Song 4: Late evening (11pm), club bathroom. Confiding in strangers: "I need this night to be good."

Song 5: Night (1am), on the dance floor. Watching the person they're crushing on flirt with someone else.

Act II

Song 6: Next morning (10am), coffee shop. Still in last night's clothes. Consoling a friend.

Song 7: Late morning (11am), outside house. Friend drops them off.

Song 8: Early afternoon (1pm), bedroom. Can't sleep—too wired.

Song 9: Late afternoon (5pm), kitchen. Thought they'd stay in, but a friend convinces them to go out again.

Song 10: Night (11pm), back at the club. Crush bumps into them. They flirt. They kiss.

Intermission

Act III

Song 11: Late night (1am), parking lot. Waiting for a text that doesn't come.

Song 12: Night (1:30am), back in the club. Crush is kissing someone else.

Song 13: Early morning (3am), bedroom. Singer is with someone else now.
Song 14: Morning (5am), bathroom. Finally gets a text from the crush.

Encore
Song 15: Morning (7am), a different bedroom. They're in bed with the person they've been chasing all along.

Yes, it's basic. Yes, it's pop. But drop any decent album into this kind of emotional map—and suddenly, you're not just playing songs. You're telling a story. You have a show.

Now add in the details I mentioned earlier (indoor or outdoor, standing or sitting) and you will quickly form a list of props, set pieces, and costumes that match those scenes.

Creating Peaks, Valleys, and Encores

Now that we've done the groundwork—first, by assigning a single emotional word to each song (along with noting its musical key), and second, by shaping the overall arc of the night and identifying where breaks, transitions, and energy shifts need to live—we're ready for the next step: placing the songs. This is where it all starts to come together. We're not just sequencing tracks. We're threading feelings, keys, and narrative tension into a living structure. In this section, we're going to build the actual setlist—slotting each song and its associated emotional goal into the architecture we've already designed—so that the show doesn't just sound good, it feels inevitable.

There are three classic setlist structures you should have in your back pocket before you invent your own. These aren't rules—but they're roadmaps. Tried, tested, and perfected by artists who've built stadium-sized emotional arcs night after night. Let's start with KISS. The KISS structure is pure spectacle. The show starts at maximum energy—there's a curtain drop, an announcer, pyro, and some kind of scenery that moves. It's loud, theatrical, relentless. The first song is a hit. So is the second. And the third. You stay at the top of the rollercoaster for as long as the crowd can handle it. Then, right around the halfway mark—where an intermission might live—you hit the brakes. A slow song.

Maybe two. Still popular, still recognizable, but designed to let people breathe, go to the bathroom, and buy more beer. And just as they settle, you punch the throttle again. Back to full blast. Bigger hits, bigger staging, more fire, more everything. The show ends at a peak. There is no comedown. No quiet goodbye. It's designed to feel like the Fourth of July met a monster truck rally and exploded on beat. If your artist is a showman, if they traffic in energy and iconography, this structure works.

Then there's Queen. Queen's structure is all about misdirection and slow-burn architecture. The show doesn't start with fireworks—it starts with confusion. An intro track, a shadow behind a curtain, maybe something off-stage or unexpected. The audience doesn't even realize the band is already playing until suddenly—boom—they're in it. The first song hits hard. It's high energy. It's a fan favorite. It announces the show has begun. And then—just as everyone settles into that adrenaline—the second song pulls all the way down. A ballad. Something tender, theatrical, or slow. Something KISS might have saved for a bathroom break. But Queen puts it right up front. Why? Because now the audience is off balance. They're not being served a linear ramp of energy—they're being drawn into a story. From there, the show builds. Slowly, strategically, moment by moment. Each section climbing a little higher, gaining weight, scale, emotion. By the time the final peak hits—usually in the last few songs—it feels earned. You've been on a journey. You've climbed. And now you're flying.

Finally, there's the Dave Matthews Band—masters of the long, slow build. This structure is all about patience. The show doesn't "start" so much as emerge. Often, the lead singer just walks onstage quietly, maybe even looking a little confused, like he wandered into the wrong building. The first notes are hesitant. Fragmented. A single riff. A long pause. Maybe some tuning. The audience leans in—not because something loud is happening, but because nothing is. And then, gradually, the show begins to rise. Not in a straight line, but in a gentle curve. One song bleeds into the next. Tempos increase. The lights expand. The band opens up. It feels organic, improvised, like a jam session that's slowly discovering itself in real time. Eventually, you realize you're in the middle of something enormous. Then there's an actual intermission—a real, full stop. And when they come back? They do it again. Same curve. Same patience. Same feeling of watching a storm roll in from the horizon. This structure works when the artist doesn't need to announce their presence, but instead invites the audience to slowly find them.

There are thousands of artists doing thousands of shows in thousands of ways—but most of them, whether they know it or not, are leaning on one of these three classic structures: the spectacle of KISS, the emotional arc of Queen, or the slow-build intimacy of Dave Matthews Band. These are the bones. The shape underneath the flash. And they work. Each of these acts developed their style from someone or somewhere else, of course—but I use them as shorthand because they're easy to research, and studying what they did will help you understand the structure behind the show.

If your artist is new, maybe with only one album under their belt—and the crowd already knows every song—it can be really tempting to take shortcuts. To phone it in. After all, the audience is probably young, eager, excited just to be there. Their expectations are low. Most people in this situation throw up a few lights, run through the record, and call it a show. But those kids? They bring their parents. And those parents have seen things. They get bored fast. So you're not just building a concert for superfans—you're building an experience that works for everyone in the room. The kids. The parents. The ushers. The bartenders. The security guards. You want them all walking out saying, "That was a real show." Not just loud. Not just cute. Real. So don't coast. Don't lean on the newness of the artist as an excuse not to do the work. Do the work anyway. Set the bar. Then raise it.

Chapter 5
Staging and Blocking for Musicians

Where to Place Performers and Why It Matters

Let's start with the elephant in the room—or rather, the riser.

If you're directing a band, odds are the drummer is sitting on top of the single biggest, bulkiest object in your world: the drum riser. If you're in pop, that same gravitational force might be a hidden drum kit stage left, or a DJ booth perched just inside the wings. If you're in hip hop, it's the DJ dead center with a laptop altar. It doesn't matter what genre you're working in—there's always one piece of gear that eats up real estate and dictates where everything else lives. That's your anchor.

Why? Because the riser is two things at once: the hardest thing to move, and the hardest thing to ignore. It's the anchor. Physically, nothing else on stage requires as much coordination to shift. You're talking about multiple crew members rolling a platform without jostling the kit, keeping the drummer from toppling off the throne, and making sure every cymbal, mic, and water bottle stays exactly where it belongs. And visually, unless the lead singer is spotlit while everyone else fades into shadow, the audience's eyes will always drift to the drum kit. It's a natural focal point, a gravitational pull. Even if you hide the kit off to the side, or swap it for a DJ booth or synth fortress, the same principle applies: the biggest piece of gear sets the center of attention unless you deliberately fight it.

Yes, the front-of-house engineers will groan. The monitor crew will mutter about phase issues. Someone will tell you "this isn't how it's

DOI: 10.4324/9781003679332-5

usually done." Ignore them. Their job is sound. Your job is story. If moving the riser makes the narrative breathe, you move it. End of discussion.

So here's the process:

Step one: look at the scenes you built in the last chapter. Each moment has a mood, a location, a feeling. Now, drop the riser into those scenes like it's a prop. Where does it go? Dead center upstage? Off to the side like it's eavesdropping? Pushed downstage to become a wall your vocalist can slam against? Decide. Because until you decide, the rest of the cast are floating in space.

Step two: once the riser is locked, everyone else finds their orbit.

Here's an example. Suppose the song is confrontational—anger, betrayal, teeth-bared energy. Don't put your singer front-and-center smiling at the crowd. Put them at a 45-degree angle, back to the house, staring down the drummer like they're the one who caused all this mess. Now stack the other players behind, facing the same gravitational center. The whole band becomes one body in conflict with the riser. You've created tension before a single lyric drops.

Now change the mood. Sadness, collapse, exhaustion. Suddenly the riser doesn't need confrontation—it needs contrast. Put your singer on the floor, downstage, lying parallel to that hulking box of drums. Maybe the rest of the players are barely visible, lurking in the shadows, like memories they can't quite shake. That riser just turned from a fight partner into a looming reminder of weight, pressure, inevitability.

This is blocking. Not "where should the bassist stand?" but "what gravitational field is everyone in?"

Sketch it out. Literally. Pen and paper. Digital whiteboard. Doesn't matter. Just get the shape of each scene on the page. Don't think of the riser as dead weight. Think of it as your set's spine. The hardest thing to move becomes the most powerful storytelling device you have.

Movement, Presence, and Visual Balance

Blocking isn't just about where people stand. It's about how they exist once they're there. You can place every performer in the perfect geometric arrangement, but if their presence doesn't match the moment, the whole thing collapses.

Think about it: if the song is sad, the performers can't stand there grinning like they're waiting for a photo op. Likewise, if it's supposed to be joyful, but someone's slouched in the corner looking like they'd rather be anywhere else, the audience feels the disconnect instantly. It pulls them out of the world you're building.

Every performer is a moving part of the stage picture. Their bodies, their posture, their gaze—even their stillness—are cues the audience reads without thinking. A singer sitting cross-legged on the floor doesn't just tell us "sad"; it feels sad because the physical shape matches the emotional shape. And if the rest of the band is arranged in shadow, unmoving, that absence of movement amplifies the focus.

So your job isn't only to sketch out where people go—it's to make sure their movements (or lack of them) reinforce the scene. Blocking is choreography in disguise. It's visual balance. If one person is disengaged, the picture tilts. If everyone's aligned—physically and emotionally—the audience never questions the truth of the moment.

Now let's talk about the movements themselves.

Take a five-piece band playing an upbeat song. If all five people are bouncing in place, that's a choice. The real question is: are they bouncing together, or not? That single decision changes how the audience reads the moment.

If they're uncoordinated, it can feel raw, spontaneous, almost chaotic—like joy breaking loose in real time. But if you never break that chaos, the audience starts to suspect it's just sloppy. That's where direction sneaks in. You can build in a cue—maybe at the pre-chorus, maybe in the middle eight—where suddenly two or three players lock eyes, hit the same jump, or slam the same chord in sync. For a heartbeat, the show admits: this isn't chaos, it's craft. Subconsciously, the audience knows: someone thought about this. Someone shaped it.

Flip to the other extreme: a pop group where every single song is a choreographed routine. Perfect lines, perfect arms, perfect steps. Impressive? Sure. For about 20 minutes. After that, it turns into wallpaper. The audience tunes out because there's no contrast—no oxygen in the system.

The traditional fix has been the "five personalities" trick: each member of the group gets their solo moment. The wild one, the serious one, the cute one, the mysterious one, and the virtuoso. One by one, they trot out their quirks in a designated number. The problem? It's been done so many times the seams are showing. The audience spots the formula, and once they spot it, they stop believing it. Manufactured individuality doesn't feel like character; it feels like marketing.

So what do you do? You break the pattern. You let imperfection in. You create contrast between uniformity and individuality, not by assigning stock roles, but by letting real variance live inside the staging. A single coordinated hit can feel stronger if it's surrounded by looseness. A single dancer breaking formation can feel more rebellious than a whole song written about rebellion. Movement is a tool. But like any tool, it loses impact if you never change how you use it.

The motions have to match the feeling of the scene. Nothing breaks the spell faster than watching a guitarist grinning and pogo-jumping through a solo in the middle of a song that's supposed to be devastating. Same with a pop group whose choreographer handed them a generic eight-count that has nothing to do with the actual moment of the show. Movement without meaning is noise. Every performer on stage—whether they're dancing, head-banging, or just standing in stillness—needs to know exactly how they should be moving in that scene. It's not optional, and it's not something you leave to chance.

At this point you might be shaking your head, thinking I'm being completely unrealistic about what a concert can demand. But this isn't theory—it's precedent. Look at Prince. From day one, anyone who joined his band had to take dance classes. Not optional. Not negotiable. If you were on his stage, you had to learn how to move, how to embody the groove as much as play it. Prince understood that presence isn't an accident—it's rehearsed, drilled, and woven into the DNA of the show.

Or take Phish, the poster child for improvisation. Their entire reputation is built on "anything can happen" looseness. And yet—every so often, right in the middle of a jam, the band pulls out trampolines and launches into a choreographed bounce routine. Why? Because even in a world obsessed with spontaneity, deliberate movement amplifies the magic. It proves the point: these principles aren't abstract. They work. They've always worked.

Directing Performers Who Aren't Actors

Here's the hardest part: most musicians aren't actors. They didn't sign up for blocking notes. They didn't expect to be told how to hold their bodies or where to stand when the lights hit. And if you're not careful with how you give those notes, you'll lose them—fast.

Theater directors have lived with this problem forever. Actors have egos. So do musicians. The trick is learning how to shape behavior without bruising pride. You never give a note in a way that makes someone look foolish in front of their peers. You never make it sound like they "did it wrong." Instead, you frame everything as service to the show.

Don't say: "You look awkward standing like that."
Say: "If you shift your weight forward during that verse, it'll read stronger from the audience."

Don't say: "You're not moving enough."
Say: "When you step downstage on that chorus, it'll connect the energy directly to the crowd."

It's a small shift, but it matters. You're not criticizing them; you're giving them tools.

Another rule from theater: always give the note privately if it's sensitive. Nothing tanks morale faster than being corrected in front of the entire band. Save the group notes for group adjustments—"Hey everyone, let's tighten the spacing on this entrance." But if it's about someone's body, posture, or vibe, pull them aside. One-on-one. Quiet. Respectful.

And remember: not every performer has the same level of self-awareness. Some need concrete, physical instructions ("Face the drummer at this point, then take three steps downstage"), while others respond better to images or feelings ("Play this verse like you're trying to shake someone off your back"). A good director adapts the note to the player.

There's another problem you'll run into, and it's so common that most people don't even clock it as a problem anymore: the unnecessary backup dancers. This whole tradition didn't start because the medium needed it—it started because Madonna wanted her music videos to look like MGM musicals. She was a dancer first, not a singer, and she built her visual identity around choreography. When it came time to tour, the shows had to resemble the videos, so the dancers came with her. And because her tours were successful, everyone else copied the template. Debbie Gibson, Paula Abdul, Janet Jackson—each iteration reinforcing the idea that a pop show requires a small army of bodies moving behind the star. That logic persists today, long after its purpose evaporated.

You get these productions where six, eight, sometimes ten dancers crowd the stage, making it hard to tell who the artist even is. What almost never gets asked is the simplest question: does the show actually need dancers? Most of the time, the answer is no. They're not there for dramaturgy; they're there because someone assumed they were mandatory. It's a habit masquerading as craft. A crutch. And at this point, it's a dated one. If movement doesn't serve the world, the moment, or the meaning, then it's just noise—and the medium has more than enough noise already.

The goal isn't to turn musicians into actors. The goal is to make them present. To make their bodies as intentional as their sound. And if you give notes with clarity, respect, and a little finesse, they'll trust you enough to follow. That trust is the difference between a concert that looks like rehearsal footage and a concert that feels like theater.

Chapter 6
Lighting that Tells a Story

Basic Lighting Principles Borrowed from Theater

In the concert world, lighting designers often drift into the role of unofficial sales representatives for the equipment manufacturers. Touring is the rare moment when they have the freedom to experiment with the latest fixtures, consoles, and effects—so they show them off. A new automated beam or laser trick appears on one major tour and, within six months, it echoes across countless others. When the effect is particularly bold, fans and critics start whispering about who copied whom. None of this has much to do with the art of serving the show. It's more about showing off what's possible than asking what's necessary.

The fundamentals of stage lighting are much simpler than the catalogs suggest. At the core, you have spotlights and follow spots—the tight, focused beams that cut through everything else to isolate a performer. These are the tools that make the singer's eyes visible in an arena, or that let a single guitar solo stand out in a sea of moving bodies. Their power lies in precision: a follow spot tracks movement, while a fixed spot locks down a moment.

Floodlights, by contrast, are broad strokes. They wash an area with color or brightness, giving shape to the stage picture without much detail. Floods can make a stage feel enormous, or they can flatten it out entirely if overused. In between, you have highlights—smaller touches of light used to pull focus subtly, the equivalent of underlining a phrase in a book rather than shouting it aloud.

DOI: 10.4324/9781003679332-6

This is the bare vocabulary a director needs to speak with a lighting designer. You don't need to know how to patch a rig or program a console. You just need to know how to ask for a follow spot on the drummer during the outro, or a flood of warm light to open up a chorus. Think of it as learning just enough words in a language to order a meal—you won't be writing poetry, but you'll get what you need.

For a director, the core lighting vocabulary comes down to a handful of fixtures. Follow spots are manually operated beams that track performers, crucial for solos and entrances. Ellipsoidals (or profile spots) give sharp, controllable beams, often used to frame key areas or project shapes. PAR cans and floodlights deliver wide washes of color, filling space and building atmosphere. Fresnels provide softer-edged light, useful for general coverage or blending between looks. Moving lights (automated spot or wash fixtures) add flexibility, shifting position, color, and texture mid-song. And finally, strobes and effects units offer intensity and spectacle, best used sparingly. With just these six categories in mind, a director can communicate effectively with a lighting designer without drowning in technical detail.

As technology evolves, the specific gear on a tour changes constantly—today it's LED washes and pixel-mapped battens, tomorrow it will be something else. Consoles get smarter, fixtures get smaller and brighter, and whole rigs can shift with the tap of a touchscreen. But those details belong to the technicians. What matters for a director is understanding the fundamentals: spots for focus, floods for breadth, washes for mood, and effects for punctuation. If you can talk in those terms, your lighting director can translate them into whatever tools are available. That's all you need to care about right now—composition, clarity, and storytelling through light.

One of the first problems you'll run into when working with lights is performers complaining that the beams are in their eyes. They'll say they can't see the audience, that the glare keeps them from "rocking," that it kills their energy. This is where you have to go back to the core principle we laid out at the start: everyone must be on the same page. When you're on stage, you're in a theater, no matter the size of the venue. Theater is about suspending reality for the audience—not for the performer. The performer's job is to serve that illusion, even when it's uncomfortable.

Any performer who believes the show should primarily be for their own enjoyment is still living in a fairy tale. There will be moments when it doesn't feel good—when the lights are blinding, when the costume itches, when the blocking feels awkward. That's part of the work. Performance is not about indulging yourself; it's about creating a world for the audience to inhabit. If the lighting is designed to deliver the story, then standing in that light is the responsibility of the performer, whether it feels good to them or not.

Another common problem is the obsession with constant movement. For some reason, many concert lighting directors feel the lights should always be in motion—sweeping, spinning, chasing—simply because they can. But when every cue moves, movement stops having meaning. It becomes wallpaper. The real power of a moving light comes when it is used sparingly and deliberately. If you have 15 scenes and 13 of them are lit with still, composed looks, then the 2 that introduce motion suddenly carry enormous weight. For example, imagine the car-in-the-parking-lot scene: rather than flooding the stage with spinning beams, you place slow-moving lights offstage to mimic the passing headlights of other cars. That motion tells a story. It builds atmosphere. It matters. By contrast, a random disco chase in the middle of a ballad only undercuts the show. Movement should always serve the narrative, not the ego of the operator.

The third major issue in concert lighting is the complete neglect of transitions. In too many shows, the lights simply snap to black after a song, the stage resets in the dark, and then the lights come back up for the next number. Sometimes designers try to paper over this with video content, but when the screen is massive and bright, it ends up washing the entire stage in whatever image is projected above it—turning the performance space into a giant glowing bulb that makes no visual sense. Transitions are not filler; they are part of the storytelling. Just as you map out each scene and its emotional palette, you must also map out how you will move from one moment to the next. That means working with your lighting designer to plan transitions as carefully as you plan cues. A fade, a shift of color, a silhouette, or a gradual crossfade can carry the audience seamlessly into the next scene, keeping them inside the world of the show rather than dumping them into dead air between songs.

The fourth and final consideration, which should be obvious by now, is that the lighting equipment itself should never be treated as part of the set—unless it is absolutely, positively necessary. Trusses, fixtures, and rigging are not scenery. When the audience can see the machinery, their suspension of disbelief begins to break down. The best lighting is invisible in its mechanics and visible only in its effect. If a fixture must be exposed, it should be intentional and motivated, not just the byproduct of laziness or convenience. Otherwise, the hardware should melt away into the background, leaving only the light itself to shape the story. And really, nothing is more absurd than watching an artist step onstage to sing a polished pop song, only to look like they're performing in the middle of an industrial yard full of scaffolding.

Designing for Impact, not just Flash

The most common mistake in concert lighting is treating it as a layer of spectacle floating above the stage, rather than as part of the architecture itself. Light isn't separate from the set—it is part of the set. The stage picture comes alive when lighting and physical elements are integrated, each shaping the other. If your budget is small and your "set" is no more than a few chairs and some painted cardboard boxes, lighting is the tool that can transform that into something larger than life. Angles, shadows, and washes can give those boxes depth, or make that chair look like it belongs in a cathedral instead of a basement. That's the real power of concert lighting: not just showing off beams and colors, but extending the physical space into something atmospheric and believable. Think less about pointing lights at performers and more about how those performers inhabit a world you build with light. When you treat light as architecture, the stage stops being a platform and starts becoming a place.

With that in mind, lighting has to follow the same logic as the rest of the show. You already know the mood you want the audience to feel, you know where the scene takes place, and whether it's meant to be indoors, outdoors, daytime, or night. All of that information must be reflected in the lighting. This isn't about someone tapping buttons in time with the beat because they think it looks flashy—it's about serving the world you've created. Too often, touring shows fall into the trap of treating lighting as a stand-alone concert gimmick. The result is beams and color chases that have no relationship to the story unfolding on stage, and once you notice the disconnect, it makes the entire show feel hollow and unwatchable. As a director, your responsibility is to insist that the lights are woven into the fabric of each scene. They are part of the composition, part of the storytelling, not an add-on. When the lighting matches the theme, the audience doesn't just watch the performance—they inhabit it.

Another key consideration is negative space—the empty areas of the stage that inevitably shift as the show plays in venues of different sizes. A set that feels tight and immersive in a small theater can suddenly look sparse and underwhelming in a large arena. The cheapest and most effective way to manage that space is with lighting. Shadows, washes, and beams can carve the stage into smaller, more intentional frames, masking the emptiness and redirecting the audience's eye where you want it. Instead of leaving those gaps to expose the limits of your production, use light to define the edges, to fill the void, or to dissolve it into darkness. Done well, lighting turns negative space into active space, making the stage feel designed no matter the scale of the venue.

If these ideas feel too abstract, the simplest solution is to borrow from reality. Start with reference images. For example, if your scene is set in a bedroom, pull up a photograph of one. Sit down with your lighting designer and study it: is there a lamp on the nightstand? Overhead lighting? Window light spilling across the floor? Maybe there's a thin strip of brightness seeping in from a bathroom door. Those details are your roadmap. You can copy them directly or use them as a starting point for your stage composition.

The same principle applies to a scene in a car. Real cars are full of light sources: the dome light above the seats, the soft glow from the dashboard, headlights casting forward, maybe even a distant streetlight grazing the side window. Find a photo of a car parked in a lot at the right time of day, and suddenly you have all the cues you need. Translate that visual reality into the stage lighting rig, and the audience will believe the environment. It's not about inventing something out of nothing—it's about observing the world as it really is and recreating that logic on stage.

Lighting as Emotional Architecture

Lighting doesn't just describe a space—it sculpts emotion into it. Once you've determined where the light sources belong in a scene, the next step is to decide how those lights will feel. This is where intensity and color become your architectural tools. A bedroom scene, for instance, can be lit faithfully with a table lamp and a window glow, but the emotional impact shifts entirely depending on what hues you choose. Photographer Gregory Crewdson is a master at this: his images place lights in realistic positions, yet the emotional tone they create—lonely, ominous, nostalgic—is unmistakably crafted. That's the model to follow.

On stage, the same room can communicate radically different moods depending on your choices. Imagine the singer isolated in a follow spot while the rest of the stage is washed in deep blue: the scene reads as cold, solitary, even mournful. Now picture that same scene in red—it becomes heated, intense, perhaps dangerous. Flip the contrast again: a red stage wash with a singer in a blue follow spot creates an otherworldly clash, drawing the eye to the performer while keeping the environment alive with tension. These are not arbitrary tricks; they're architectural choices that shape how the audience feels in the space you've built.

This is where your vision boards come back into play. You've already collected the images that define the emotional tone of each scene—now they become your color map. If you're unsure which shades dominate a reference photo, there are plenty of apps and websites that can extract a palette for you automatically from your vision board photos. Hand that palette to your lighting designer, and they'll know where to begin. By combining placement, mood, and color in this way, you're not guessing—you're translating a visual plan into emotional architecture.

I cannot stress this enough: if you only learn one thing from this book, it's that lighting must serve the show, not sabotage it. There is nothing more incoherent than watching a performer sing an intimate, emotionally charged ballad about heartbreak while the stage erupts in strobing chaos, as if a UFO were about to land. Sure, it feels exciting for the person standing under the lights, and it might keep the attention of an audience dulled by too many drinks—but to everyone else, it rings false. Subconsciously, the audience starts to check out because what they're seeing doesn't match what they're hearing. The emotional contract between stage and spectator breaks down.

That's why lighting cannot be treated as an afterthought or an accessory. It has to be designed hand-in-hand with the sets, as part of the same architecture. The set designer and the lighting designer must be in the room with you from the earliest stages, working as collaborators. These elements are not separate departments—they are two sides of the same design problem. A show that integrates its lighting with its environment creates a world the audience can believe in. A show that doesn't? It just looks like noise.

It may take far longer than you expect to find a lighting designer who truly understands these concepts and is willing to collaborate at that level. Many are trained to think in terms of equipment and effects, not architecture and storytelling. You may go through several before you find the one who gets it—but it is worth the wait. The entire production depends on this partnership. Without it, you're building a house with no foundation. With it, every element of the show gains coherence and power.

Chapter 7
Sound Design for Impact

The Director's Role in Audio Decisions

In concerts, sound is the invisible glue holding the performance together, and yet it is also the first thing an audience will notice if it goes wrong. Lights can flicker, a costume can tear, even a set piece can wobble and the show will survive—but if the sound collapses, so does the audience's belief in the world you've built. As a director, you don't need to become a sound engineer, but you do need to understand the roles of the two key people who shape every note that leaves the stage: the monitor engineer and the front-of-house (FOH) engineer.

The monitor engineer's job is deceptively simple: make sure the performers can hear what they need in order to stay engaged and give their best performance. In practice, this means learning every performer's quirks and preferences—who wants their voice louder than anything else, who needs to feel the bass thump in their chest, who insists on hearing the kick drum as if it were right behind their head. No two performers want the same thing, and no single night is ever identical. The monitor engineer is less an operator of equipment than a kind of caretaker of each artist's private world on stage.

This work often requires a private language between performer and engineer. Sometimes it's literal—a whispered word into a talkback mic between songs, a phrase only the two of them understand. Other times it's purely physical: a gesture, a flick of the wrist, a pantomime of turning a knob or raising a hand. Done well, this language is invisible to the audience. Done poorly, it becomes a clumsy

DOI: 10.4324/9781003679332-7

interruption, a reminder that the artifice is just a band shouting commands across a stage.

Traditionally, the monitor engineer has been stationed in the wings, surrounded by racks of equipment and visible to anyone glancing sideways from the audience. Technology has made that position obsolete. Wireless systems, remote-controlled mixing boards, and digital snakes mean there is no reason for the monitor engineer to be anywhere near the performers in sight of the crowd. The closer they are to the stage, the more likely the audience is to see them as part of the show's machinery, and that is not their role. As director, your job is to insist that they be invisible—physically out of sight and theatrically erased from the world of the performance.

Just as important is your insistence that communication between performers and the monitor engineer be hidden from the audience. A singer calling out "Can I get more vocal in my monitor?" between songs may seem harmless, but it destroys the atmosphere you've spent hours constructing. The audience is yanked out of the concert world and reminded they are watching a technical rehearsal in progress. Your responsibility is to make sure these conversations are handled silently, subtly, and seamlessly. The performers must appear to exist in their own universe; the monitor engineer must be the unseen hand keeping that illusion alive.

The moment you start treating the monitor engineer as part of your creative team rather than just another technician, you'll discover how much power they hold over the consistency and believability of the show. They are not there to showcase technology—they are there to protect the performers' ability to live inside the story you are telling. And that protection, when it works, is invisible.

Working with FOH

If the monitor engineer is responsible for sustaining the performers' world, the (FOH engineer is responsible for sustaining the audience's. They are the ones mixing the sound that fills the venue, shaping what every audience member hears and experiences. But unlike the monitor engineer, who can be invisible, the FOH engineer cannot be hidden. They sit in the middle of the audience, a physical presence within the theatrical space. That presence matters—and too often it is overlooked. The essential difference is this: the monitor engineer is best when invisible, while the FOH engineer inevitably performs a double role—both technician and, whether they like it or not, part of the cast.

Because the FOH engineer is visible, they are, whether anyone admits it or not, part of the show. Their costume, their posture, their mannerisms, even the way they speak to audience members who ask them questions—all of it contributes to the atmosphere you've worked so hard to create. Imagine staging a concert in a carefully designed 17th-century castle, only for your FOH engineer to sit dead center in jeans and a club t-shirt. The illusion collapses. For the audience, the castle evaporates and they are reminded they are just standing in a modern arena.

The same is true of the equipment. Racks of gear, glowing screens, metal barricades—they may be necessary, but they do not have to be disruptive. Just as you would costume a performer, you should costume the sound booth. Hide the technology as much as possible, or at least frame it within the world of the production. A castle does not need a steel barricade; it needs a draped partition, a wooden rail, something that belongs to the story. The audience should never have to reconcile a 21st-century aluminum truss with the 17th-century world you have promised them.

This extends to the venue itself. Many spaces come with advertising slapped across the walls or branded banners plastered over the stage. Left alone, they fight against your design. A soda logo glowing in the background of a torchlit medieval hall is absurd, but it happens all the time. The solution is not to shrug but to plan for it in advance. In your earliest design conversations, when you mapped how the show would adapt to different venues, you should have considered how to disguise or reframe these intrusions. If you don't, they will sabotage you at the moment when you can least afford it: in front of a paying audience.

The FOH engineer's mix may be their main responsibility, but their presence is yours. As director, it is up to you to ensure that everything the audience sees and hears matches the world you've built. That includes the person in the middle of the room riding the faders.

Another thing to understand about the FOH engineer is their rhythm of work. They are often busiest when everyone else is waiting, and waiting when everyone else is busy. During soundcheck they are frantically shaping the balance, while stagehands stand idle; during the show they may have long stretches of steady mixing with little to do while the crew backstage is scrambling. Because of this imbalance, FOH engineers are more likely than other team members to invite guests to "hang out" at the booth—or even let them watch the show from that position. What seems harmless camaraderie backstage becomes a distraction for the audience. A booth crowded with friends scrolling on phones or whispering to each other is just as disruptive to the illusion as an out-of-place prop on stage.

The same principle applies to direct audience interactions. Audience members will often approach the FOH engineer with questions: Where's the restroom? What time does the band go on? Can you turn it down? If the answers are casual or inconsistent, the illusion cracks again. As director, you should anticipate this. Work with the FOH engineer to identify the most common questions they receive, and then script answers that are both practical and thematic. Rehearse them the way you would rehearse a line of dialogue. A guest who asks, "When's the encore?" in your imagined 17th-century castle should not be answered with, "I don't know, probably 10:30." Instead, the response might be, "The lords of the castle have not yet decreed the final summons, but you may expect the hall to stir again before the night grows too dark." Done well, this transforms an interruption into an extension of the show itself—easier for the engineer, and more memorable for the audience.

Finally, your relationship with the FOH engineer begins long before the audience arrives. In the earliest planning stages of the show, you must collaborate with them to make sure the production isn't burdened with unnecessary complications. One of the most common pitfalls is wireless technology. Every new tour seems to demand more wireless devices—microphones, in-ears, instruments, talkbacks—until the airwaves are saturated. Each additional frequency is one more potential failure point, one more interference risk, and one more distraction for the engineer. As director, your responsibility is to question whether the convenience of a wireless device is worth the risk. A cleverly disguised microphone may look seamless on stage, but does it need to be wireless at all? If a cable can achieve the same effect invisibly, the simplest solution is often the strongest.

The same discipline applies to the question of guitar pedals. Some acts treat pedalboards as an extension of their identity, cycling through a new effect on every song until the stage is littered with boxes, cables, and blinking lights. Fifteen pedals may give a guitarist freedom, but for the audience they can be a visual intrusion—an accidental second set design that undercuts your world. As director, you should not accept this at face value. Work with both the FOH engineer and the performers to decide what is truly necessary. If a variety of sounds is essential, explore alternatives. Can a guitar tech trigger pedals offstage? If the effects are digital, can they be consolidated into a single unit triggered by someone else at the appropriate time? Can the board itself be hidden, masked, or integrated into the design so that it supports rather than sabotages the story?

The FOH engineer is not just a sound operator but a partner in world-building. Their technical expertise and your aesthetic discipline must align. Left unchecked, gear and gadgets multiply until the show becomes an advertisement for technology rather than an environment for storytelling. When you plan early and rigorously with the FOH engineer, you ensure that sound design enhances the illusion rather than exposing its seams.

How Sound Can Cue Emotional Transitions

If light is the architecture of space, then sound is the architecture of time. Every shift in music or tone tells the audience where they are not only physically but emotionally. The first place this becomes apparent is before the show even begins. The pre-show soundtrack is often treated as filler, but in reality it is the audience's first step into the world you have built.

What does the audience hear when they walk into the room? If they are greeted with a random playlist of popular songs, you have already weakened your illusion. Worse still are songs from an entirely different genre, or songs too similar to the ones the audience is about to hear—both remind them of Spotify, not of the world of your show. On the other hand, well-chosen pre-show music can draw them in before a single performer steps on stage. Environmental sounds that match the location—waves crashing, birds in the forest, city traffic in the distance—can transport the audience immediately. Instrumental or "chill" versions of the artist's own songs can create a sense of familiarity without undercutting the performance to come. Rare demos or unreleased tracks, if played at a reasonable volume, can make even the waiting feel like a privileged part of the experience.

Volume is as much a tool as content. The common practice is to start quiet and gradually raise the level until the show begins, which can work—but only if it matches your setlist. If the first song is explosive, then priming the audience with a slow crescendo makes sense. But if the show opens on a low note and builds gradually, why exhaust the audience before it even starts? Consider the nature of the crowd as well: are they a social audience who enjoy chatting until the lights go down, or an introspective one who needs space to settle into silence? Your sound choices must shape their emotional state, not fight against it.

You must also decide whether there is a pre-show performance element. A costumed character wandering the aisles, an ambient video loop, or a subtle soundscape piped into the lobby all demand different sound strategies. Ignoring this means losing control of the first ten minutes of your show—minutes in which the audience is most ready to be transported.

And just as important as how they enter is how they leave. Exit music should be given as much thought as pre-show music. Do you want the audience to leave elated, lingering, buzzing with energy? Or do you want them hushed, reflective, carrying the atmosphere home in silence? A triumphant finale undercut by generic pop blasting over the PA is an incoherent ending. By planning the exit as carefully as the entrance, you extend the story beyond the last note of the encore, sending the audience back into the world still under the spell of the one you created.

This is also the part of the show where the FOH engineer most visibly becomes part of the cast. Unlike the monitor engineer, whose work is largely hidden once the performance begins, the FOH engineer is actively shaping the audience's emotional state in real time. Doors rarely open and the show begins on a fixed schedule without variation. Sometimes there are long stretches to fill before the band takes the stage, sometimes things run late, sometimes a support act cancels, and occasionally the headliner must start earlier than planned.

In these moments, the FOH engineer is not just playing a playlist—they are manipulating mood like a DJ, extending or shortening tracks, looping environmental sounds, or even crossfading into higher or lower energy music depending on what is happening backstage. If the band is delayed, the FOH engineer's role is to sustain anticipation without exhausting the crowd. If the show must start early, they need to accelerate the build-up smoothly so the audience is ready for the first note.

As director, your task is to prepare them for this role. Do not hand over a fixed playlist and hope for the best. Instead, treat the pre- and post-show recordings as flexible materials. Script the emotional journey in broad strokes, and then rehearse with the FOH engineer how to adjust those strokes in real time. They are performers in their own right, guiding the audience through the unpredictable gaps and delays that live performance always contains. If they are unprepared, the illusion falters. If they are ready, the audience never notices the machinery; they only feel the world of the show holding them from first step in the door to final step out into the night.

The final element to consider is how sound transitions between songs. Many engineers will tell you it takes the first three numbers of a set to fully "dial in" the mix, because the acoustics of a room shift dramatically once it fills with bodies. An empty hall is not the same as a hall alive with thousands of breathing, moving people. The FOH engineer must therefore make subtle adjustments in those opening songs, gradually shaping the sound to its true balance. As director, you should not fight this reality—you should design for it. Accept that the first few songs are part of a sonic transition, and build your setlist accordingly. Do not place your most fragile moment second, when the sound is still settling. Give your engineer space to stabilize before asking the audience to lean in.

Once the mix has found its balance, protect it. Nothing is more disruptive than snapping the audience's ears back to zero with a jarring non-musical interruption. A blaring video, an unplanned announcement, or a sudden cut to silence between songs forces the crowd to recalibrate every time, breaking the arc you are working so carefully to construct. Between-song elements should carry the audience forward, not throw them sideways. Continuity is everything: once you have led the audience into the world, every sonic choice must keep them there.

And this is where one of the trickiest real-world problems often appears: promoters and sponsors who insist on making announcements. Almost every director has faced the dreaded moment when someone in street clothes wanders on stage and starts reading a list of upcoming shows, thanking a car dealership, or plugging the bar. Nothing destroys your carefully built illusion faster. You cannot always say no—but you can prepare. Plan for it early in the production process. Decide where that announcer will be, costume them appropriately, and give them a script that allows them to weave the necessary information into the world of the show. If you know it's coming, you can fold it into the architecture of the event rather than letting it smash through the walls.

The FOH engineer is central here as well. They will be responsible for cueing the microphone, setting the volume, and ensuring the announcement blends into the soundscape rather than standing apart from it. If you bring them into the planning from the start, they can help ensure that even this unwanted intrusion serves the story instead of sabotaging it.

If you take only one thing away from this chapter, let it be this: sound must serve the story, not impede it. Every choice—from the pre-show music to the last word of an encore, from the FOH engineer's presence to the whisper of a monitor cue—either reinforces the world you've built or tears it apart. The audience will forgive a late start, a dropped note, even a missed light cue. But if the sound breaks the illusion, the spell is gone. Your responsibility as director is to make sure every sonic element, whether heard or merely seen in its delivery, belongs to the architecture of your show. Done with care, sound does not just carry the music—it carries the audience into the story and holds them there until the very end.

Chapter 8

Visuals, Screens, and Multimedia

Integrating Visuals without Distracting from the Artist

The concert stage is not an accident of architecture. For centuries, thespians, playwrights, and directors experimented with circles, thrusts, and multi-sided spaces before finally settling on the rectangle—not because it was simpler, but because it gave them control. A rectangular frame allows directors and designers to create perspective, to conceal machinery, and to focus the audience's attention in one direction. The proscenium is, in effect, a giant picture frame. That frame is not neutral. It tells the audience where to look and it gives you, as director, a canvas.

In a concert, this matters more than ever. Screens, projections, and LED walls now dominate the edges of that rectangle. Used well, they extend the stage, amplifying the story and guiding emotion. Used badly, they compete with the performer, pulling the audience's gaze away from the human center of the show. The question you must ask is not, "Can I fill this rectangle with visuals?" but "How can I shape it so every pixel serves the artist?"

The first thing to accept about screens is that they are magnets. No matter how powerful your performer, the human eye will always be pulled toward a glowing rectangle. If you place a giant LED wall behind your singer, you are already creating a competition. Unless the visuals are handled carefully, the audience stops attending to the live body in front of them and starts watching television. You have not staged a concert—you have staged a viewing party.

DOI: 10.4324/9781003679332-8

A better model is the game show. Think about how screens are used there: not as rivals to the host, but as extensions of the host's role. The contestant presses a button and the board lights up. The host gestures toward the display and the audience's eyes follow, then return immediately to the person on stage. The technology serves the human moment, never eclipses it. That should be your aim with concert screens. The screen should breathe with the performer, react to them, and expand their presence—not smother it.

There is another trap: cameras. A lens at the front of the stage, or worse, a boom arm swinging into view, instantly shifts the audience's perception. They are no longer at a concert; they are at a television taping. The energy changes. Instead of immersion in the world you've built, they begin to wonder which angle they'll see on the jumbotron. As director, you must guard against this. Cameras are not neutral tools—they are actors on stage, and unless you costume and choreograph them as part of the world, they will betray the illusion.

Go back to our earlier example of a 17th-century castle. If that is the world you are building, there is no place for a video screen. A glowing wall of pixels immediately collapses the illusion—your medieval hall vanishes and you are left with a rock band playing in front of a Best Buy showroom. The simple rule is: if the world you are creating does not logically contain a screen, do not bring one in.

Of course, reality is rarely so clean. Many venues come with permanent screens you cannot remove or turn off. In those cases, your responsibility is not to surrender but to adapt. Treat the screens the way you would treat a stray soda logo on the wall: disguise it, reframe it, or fold it into your aesthetic. Stock footage is your friend here. If you are trapped with LED panels, do not leave them blank or let them run advertisements between acts. Fill them with imagery that belongs to your world: forests swaying in the wind, birds crossing the sky, torches flickering in the night. Even generic atmospheric textures are better than the harsh reminder of modern hardware. Done well, the screens stop being intrusions and instead become moving scenery, silent partners in sustaining the story of your castle.

Storyboarding Visuals and Projections

By the time you reach visuals, you already have a skeleton: the setlist arc, the mood words, the staging diagrams, and the lighting story. What storyboarding does is put skin on that skeleton. It ties the screen content and the stage action together into one picture, making sure the digital world and the live world move in the same rhythm.

This is why you can't stop at a single storyboard. One board shows the screen alone—the moving images, the projections, the live feed cues. The other shows the stage with the screen included, because the performer's body and the digital frame are inseparable. If you design one without the other, you end up with two parallel shows fighting each other for the audience's attention.

Think of the dual boards as two halves of a conversation.

The Screen Board asks: What story is the screen telling on its own? What fills it—video, texture, color, blackness? How does it change over the course of the verse, the chorus, the bridge? Where does it hold still, and where does it erupt?

The Stage Board asks: How do the humans respond to that story? Where does the performer stand in relation to the screen? Are they framed by it, dwarfed by it, silhouetted against it? Is the screen echoing their movement or contradicting it? What is the shape of the screen? Where is it located on (or off) of the stage?

When you build both boards side by side, you start to see how the concert breathes as a whole. The screen stops being a TV in the background and becomes a partner in staging. And remember: a screen doesn't have to be a giant rectangle upstage. With projection mapping, it can be fractured into set pieces, wrapped around columns, or spread across the floor like an illuminated carpet. It can live in the wings, or in the ceiling, or in the shape of a window or doorway. Sometimes it's the entire environment; other times it's just a sliver—a flicker of light on the edge of the scene. The point is that the screen is not a fixed box. It is a material. A surface. A canvas that can be shaped to the world you're building. Once you stop treating it like a television and start treating it like scenery, you unlock its power.

The process looks like this:

First, start with your emotional map. You already have one word per song from your vision boards. That word is the anchor for both the screen and the stage. If the word is "longing," the screen might hold an endless horizon, while the performer stays isolated downstage. If the word is "rage," the screen might fracture into shards while the band crowds center stage.

Second, storyboard the screen's beats. Treat it like a short film, broken into moments that align with the musical structure. Don't think in terms of "what would look cool"—think in terms of what the emotion requires.

Third, overlay the stage. Place the riser, the performers, the lighting states. Sketch how they inhabit or resist the imagery. Remember: silence and stillness apply here too. A blank screen can be as powerful as an explosion of visuals—sometimes more.

Finally rehearse the interaction. Just as you would rehearse a blocking cue or a lighting state, rehearse how the performers live with the screen. A hand gesture timed to a projection change, a pause while the screen resolves into black—these are not accidents. They're choreography between flesh and pixels.

One of the easiest ways to derail your visual world is by putting actors into the videos. The moment you do, the audience stops watching the performer on stage and starts asking: Who is this new character? What are they doing here? Are they part of the story? Instead of deepening the world, you've introduced a distraction. Unless your entire concept is built around integrating film characters with live performance, keep your screens actor-free. Let the visuals serve the performer, not compete with them.

Another pitfall is inconsistency. Why are we watching a black-and-white newsreel from the 1920s in one song and a grainy 1970s suspense film in the next? These stylistic clashes don't read as clever variety—they read as incoherence. Color grading is part of your visual language, and like any language, it needs consistency. Once you've built a world, every image must belong to it. Jarring shifts in palette can undo the spell you've worked so hard to build.

Be wary of leaning on CGI and animation. They may look slick in the moment, but technology and style age faster than almost anything else. What looks "cutting-edge" today will look painfully dated when the concert is revisited on video ten years from now. If you must use animation, ground it in simplicity and timelessness—shapes, textures, movement—rather than the hyper-stylized trends of the moment.

Another choice that reveals a director's hand is how the show begins. Visuals at the top set the tone, which is why tacky openings are so destructive. Avoid the cliché of following the artist from the dressing room to the stage. Avoid the "mystical obstacle course" video that promises the artist will "overcome" something before they sing a single note. And above all, avoid the dreaded backstory montage that tells the audience how famous and important the artist already is. They bought the ticket. They know. The job of the opening visuals is not to explain—it's to immerse.

Finally, be ruthless about quality control. Bad typography, canned stock audio, and generic production cues can unravel everything else you've built. A single cheesy font or mismatched sound effect reminds the audience they're watching filler, not theater. The screen should be treated with the same rigor as the set, the lights, or the costumes. Every frame, every word, every sound has to feel like it belongs to the same world. Anything less breaks the illusion.

A holistic storyboard is not just a planning tool—it's a guarantee. It ensures that the video designer, the lighting operator, the camera crew, and the performers are all telling the same story. Without it, you get what most tours default to: a playlist running in the background while the band plays in the foreground. With it, you get a unified stage picture—digital and physical fused into one coherent world.

Syncing Visual Elements with Live Cues

The biggest trap with visuals is treating them like a film—perfectly locked, frame by frame, no air, no give. That may look clean on paper, but in practice it kills the show. A concert is a living thing. Tempos shift, performers stretch moments, audiences push the energy in directions no one predicted. If your visuals are welded to timecode, every deviation becomes a mistake. The band leans into the chorus a few beats longer, and suddenly the video is already halfway through the bridge. The illusion cracks.

The solution is human control. Visuals should be triggered live, by a VJ, projectionist, or operator who is watching the performers in real time. That person becomes another musician—part of the band, even if they're sitting behind a console instead of a guitar. Their job is not to hit "play" on a pre-rendered film but to breathe with the show, shaping the visuals to the same pulse the performers are following.

That doesn't mean chaos. You don't need every second mapped. What you need are key points—a handful of beats in each song where the visuals and the performers lock together perfectly. A blackout timed to a crash. A burst of imagery that lands on the downbeat. A dissolve that carries the emotional lift of a chorus. If those anchors are rehearsed and flawless, they compensate for every minor variation around them. The audience won't notice tiny slips; they will only feel the precision where it matters most.

And here's the bonus: leaving wiggle room makes the show feel more alive. A perfectly repeatable sequence can turn into wallpaper after the second or third viewing. But when visuals flex with the performance—when they feel like they are breathing with the singer instead of playing over them—the show gains a sense of uniqueness. It doesn't look like a film running behind a concert; it looks like a concert that could only happen tonight, in this room, with this audience.

That's the balance to aim for: freedom framed by anchors. Not every moment needs to sync. But the ones that do must be airtight, rehearsed until the operator and the performers move as one. Between those anchors, let the visuals drift, expand, contract, respond. That's where the life is.

A lazy mistake most shows make is to throw a looping visual on screen and let it run from the start of the song until the end. It's easy, it fills the rectangle, and it gives the illusion of design—but it's not direction. The audience may not know the mechanics, but they feel the repetition. A loop doesn't respond to the performer. It doesn't shift when the chorus lands, it doesn't breathe with the bridge, it doesn't fall silent at the right moment. It just sits there, chewing time.

The danger is subtle: the loop teaches the audience that the screen is wallpaper. Once they stop paying attention to it, the screen loses its power. Worse, when you actually do want a screen moment to land, it feels no different than the filler that came before. Every frame should earn its place. If you don't have a reason for the image to be there, black is better. A blank screen creates space, anticipation, and focus—while a loop just burns the audience's patience.

Chapter 9
Costumes
From Concept to Quick Change

One Visual Language, not Three

Hair, makeup, and costume are not three separate departments—they are one language. On stage, the audience does not parse them individually; they register the total impression. A gown paired with the wrong hairstyle collapses into parody, just as flawless tailoring undermined by clumsy makeup reads as amateur. As director, you must think of them as facets of the same character, the same world. For each character, you must understand that each of these skills (hair, makeup, and costume) is its own discipline, while still performing the role of a stylist to ensure that the three mediums are coordinated.

The silhouette, the skin, the color palette—these are all strokes of the same brush. A singer's smoky eye, a leather jacket, and a slicked-back ponytail together create a single line of meaning; swap the ponytail for loose curls and the line changes. Every detail, from the heel height to the eyeliner thickness, contributes to the same sentence. If you delegate them as separate errands—"the costume designer handles the clothes, the stylist handles the hair, the makeup artist handles the face"—you risk three voices speaking in three dialects. Your task is to fuse them so the performer steps on stage as one complete image, seamless, inevitable, undeniable.

A costume is not just an image—it is a tool. However dazzling it may appear under the lights, if the performer cannot move, breathe, or sing in it, the costume has failed. Your job as director is not to design the garment yourself but to communicate clearly what the performer needs

DOI: 10.4324/9781003679332-9

to do in it. Will they be climbing a riser, crouching with a guitar, leaping into the crowd, or simply standing in stillness for ten minutes under a follow spot? Each of these actions demands a different kind of construction, fabric, and flexibility.

A suit of armor that looks magnificent from the tenth row but restricts arm movement will ruin a solo. A gown that sparkles on camera but traps the singer's diaphragm will strangle a note. Even shoes are narrative devices: the wrong heel height can change posture, gait, and energy, shifting the meaning of a song. The costume designer cannot guess these requirements—they need you to articulate them. When you provide that information early, the costume becomes more than decoration; it becomes an instrument the performer can play with freedom, seamlessly integrated into the show's physical and emotional score.

Costumes cannot be designed in isolation, and neither can hair or makeup. Just as you would never dream of developing the set without consulting the lighting designer, you must bring the hair, makeup, and costume team into those same early conversations. Fabric does not exist in a vacuum—it lives in light. A crimson jacket may glow with fire under tungsten but sink into mud under LED blue. A shimmer of glitter on the cheek may read as radiance in rehearsal and as sweat under the wrong spotlight. The set, too, changes everything: a pale backdrop can wash out pastel tones, while a dark structure can make the same palette sing with vibrancy.

If you wait until the dress rehearsal to discover these clashes, it is too late; the costume designer is forced into last-minute compromises, and the illusion cracks. Instead, insist that these teams work as one unit from the start, so color, texture, and silhouette are chosen with the stage picture in mind. This way, every gown, every hairstyle, every flick of eyeliner exists in harmony with the world the audience will actually see—not the world imagined on a sketchpad.

Everyone the Audience Sees is Part of the Picture

Costume planning begins with a list of everyone we need to costume—and that list must go far beyond the headliners. The performers may be the most obvious, but every body the audience sees contributes to the stage picture. That includes the sound engineer who is visible at front of house, the stagehands who cross the wings, and even the venue staff if they are within the world you are building.

If you are playing in clubs or bars, why not fold the bartenders into the design? A branded t-shirt, a simple apron, or even a small accessory in the show's palette can pull them into the aesthetic, making the entire environment feel curated rather than accidental. The same applies to ushers, ticket-takers, or security—anyone who might cross the audience's field of vision. Of course, budget will set limits, but the principle is simple: if the audience can see a person, that person is part of your cast. Treat them as such.

Even a minor accessory—a pin, a scarf, a sash—can erase the jarring contrast between a carefully designed stage world and a fluorescent-vested reality. By thinking inclusively, you turn the whole venue into an extension of the performance.

Build for Breakdowns, not Perfection

Redundancy is not extravagance—it's survival. Every performer needs at least two of every core costume piece, no matter how sturdy it looks in the fitting. Sweat, spilled drinks, broken zippers, torn seams, sudden rain during an outdoor encore—these things do not wait politely until after the curtain call. Nothing shatters the illusion faster than a singer sprinting offstage mid-set because their only jacket ripped down the back.

As director, it's your job to insist on duplicates. A second shirt, a backup pair of shoes, an identical dress waiting on a hanger—these are not luxuries but guarantees that the show can go on without panic. Even small items like belts, jewelry, or hats should be doubled, because the tiny things are the easiest to lose or break in the chaos of quick changes. Think of it as a safety net: the audience never sees it, but without it, the entire performance hangs by a thread. Two of everything keeps the world intact, no matter what the night throws at you.

A costume that works beautifully on stage but can't survive the road is a liability. Touring means constant packing, unpacking, and cramming wardrobes into trunks, trucks, or overhead bins, often with minutes to spare. As director, you must push for costumes that are built not only to look right but to travel well. Fabrics should resist wrinkling under pressure, seams must endure repeated folding, and designs should be practical to clean and repair on the fly. A sweeping velvet cape might look stunning in rehearsal, but if it weighs 40 pounds and requires its own suitcase, it will become a burden the crew resents.

Likewise, shoes should be chosen for durability as much as style, because they will endure hundreds of hours of walking, dancing, and waiting backstage. Think like a traveler: what folds flat, what rolls tight, what can be steamed quickly in a hotel bathroom? A costume that can be transported easily is not a compromise—it is a necessity. Without that foresight, every city on the tour becomes a fresh opportunity for disaster.

One of the most overlooked realities of costume design is the path between the dressing room and the stage. In theory, the performer steps from a pristine greenroom directly into the spotlight. In practice, they may be hustled down a stairwell, across an alley slick with rain, past dumpsters, through a working kitchen, or along a corridor lined with cables and road cases. Costumes must be built with these journeys in mind.

Long trains, fragile fabrics, and protruding elements may look magnificent under lights but become hazards the moment they brush against a swinging door or a greasy countertop. As director, you have to raise these practical questions with the costume designer early: Can the performer walk quickly in this? Will it snag on a handle? Can it survive a dash through bad weather without becoming unwearable? The designer's sketches may dazzle on paper, but your responsibility is to pressure-test them against the real, messy world of live performance. By asking these questions before final fittings, you ensure that the costume is not just beautiful in theory but functional in the unforgiving environments the performer must navigate.

The greatest trap in concert costuming is mistaking the stage for a runway—or worse, for a swimsuit ad. Too often, artists believe that showing as much skin as possible is automatically exciting, regardless of what the scene demands. The result is a strange disconnect: a singer baring midriff and legs during a ballad about grief, or a band strutting shirtless through a scene that otherwise suggests vulnerability.

There is nothing inherently wrong with revealing the body—if the scene calls for sensuality, rawness, or exposure, then skin can be a powerful tool. But when it appears without purpose, it reads as vanity rather than storytelling. Fashion for fashion's sake and nudity for nudity's sake both pull the audience out of the world you are trying to sustain.

As director, you must remind performers that the body, like the lights or the set, is one more element in the design. It should serve the scene, and the scene should serve the show. When deployed with intention, costuming—or the lack of it—can heighten emotion. When deployed without intention, it merely distracts.

Chapter 10
Audience Engagement
Energy, Eye Contact, and Euphoria

Treating the Crowd as a Character

The most common mistake directors and performers make when thinking about the audience is imagining them as a blank wall to throw energy against. They shout, they gesture, they broadcast—as if the audience were a void to be filled. But in a concert, the audience is not a void. They are a character. And like any character, they come with a perspective, a set of responses, and a role in the story you are shaping.

The difference is that this character cannot be scripted word for word. You cannot dictate how they feel or force them to think in unison. Instead, you invite them into the experience by showing them your point of view and allowing them to lean in. It is less about telling them, "This is funny, now laugh," and more about showing them what you find absurd, tragic, or beautiful—and letting them arrive at their own laughter, their own tears. The relationship is not commander to soldier but host to guest: you ask the audience to look over your shoulder, see your point of view, and show them the perspective of the show that moves you. In building the show this way, you are making the connection with the audience more personal and more effective.

This is why performers who mug for approval often break the spell. The moment the artist insists too loudly—"Do you see what I see? Isn't this hilarious?"—the audience feels pushed, not welcomed. But when the performer simply lives inside the moment with clarity, when they look at the absurdity, the irony, the joy as if sharing a secret, the audience naturally joins in. They feel they are part of something discovered, not dictated.

DOI: 10.4324/9781003679332-10

As director, your task is to coach performers to sustain that attitude. Every gesture, every pause, every look out into the house should feel like a conversation with a partner who happens to number in the thousands. Think of it as staging a scene with an invisible character—one that sits across from the performer, reacting silently. The performer is not explaining to them; they are showing them.

And when the balance is right, the crowd ceases to be a passive assembly. They become a responsive organism, breathing with the show, laughing and gasping in rhythm. They are the missing scene partner. Treat them as such, and you stop directing a broadcast. You begin directing a dialogue.

A good portion of the audience already feels like they know the performer, even though they don't, and the rest have just been introduced to them. That means part of your job as director is to calibrate how the performer onboards the crowd. You must introduce their mannerisms, their language, and their little world in a way that feels natural—without ever pausing to explain it outright.

The trick is balance: give just enough exhibition to the new people without insulting the old ones. The longtime fans don't need a glossary. They've already lived inside the artist's vocabulary for years. But the newcomers need a way in, a door that opens just wide enough to let them understand what everyone else is laughing at, or what ritual they're being swept into.

The best performers build this gradually, by doing, not by describing. Think of Dave Matthews drifting into his made-up vernacular between songs: half-stories, fragments of jokes, improvised syllables that no one outside the room could ever parse. He never stops to translate. He simply lives inside that speech pattern until the audience has no choice but to accept it as normal. Or James Brown, who turned his stage language into ritual: the cape, the kneel, the shouted call-and-response—all of it grew into a vocabulary that audiences understood instinctively over the course of the night. Neither of them paused to explain the grammar. They just used it until it became the air the crowd was breathing.

Contrast that with weaker examples: the performer who breaks the illusion to explain how their own ritual works. "When I take a step forward, everybody clap." The moment you spell it out, the magic collapses.

It shifts from discovery to instruction, from immersion to homework. Or consider Taylor Swift, after she had sold millions of records and was playing stadiums, interrupting shows with, "Hi, my name is Taylor." What might have been charming in the early days reads as self-conscious later on, as if she were introducing herself at a school assembly instead of drawing the audience into her world.

If someone likes you, they will mimic your behavior and body language. It's a basic human reflex—we mirror the people we admire. In a concert, the same principle applies, only scaled up. Instead of one-to-one, it becomes one-to-many. When the performer sways, the crowd sways. When they laugh, the crowd laughs. When they drop their voice to a whisper, thousands lean in without being told. That mimicry is not obedience—it's empathy. It's the audience entering into rhythm with the performer, not because they were instructed, but because they were invited. Harness that, and you are no longer explaining rituals. You are embodying them, and the crowd is echoing back your presence as their own.

A few common mistakes are worth pointing out. If a band does the routine of asking, "Does anyone here play guitar?" and then brings someone up from the crowd, the worst thing they can do is pick the youngest person in sight. The surprise fizzles because it feels predictable. Instead, pick the least likely candidate—the overweight, middle-aged person halfway back who looks like they've given up on life. When that person tears into a solo, the audience erupts, because the story flips from expectation to revelation. The same goes for dancing or any kind of on-stage interaction: choose the least obvious person, not the most obvious. And whatever you do, never bring up someone in costume unless that costume directly relates to the band's work. Nine times out of ten, that person isn't there for the show—they're waiting for a microphone to advertise a local business or their side project, and they will derail your performance in a heartbeat.

And finally: never bring anyone on stage who is holding a sign. Signs are almost always an audition for attention. The moment that person gets a microphone, they'll try to hijack the show by telling the performer—and the entire audience—their life story. Instead, pick the person who seems least likely to be picked. That inversion almost always pays off, because it turns surprise into joy. The crowd delights in seeing the unexpected elevated, while the sign-holder learns the hard truth: attention is earned through the show's design, not demanded with cardboard and marker.

As director, your job is to protect the performer from that impulse to overexplain. You must help them trust that their quirks, their language, their gestures will be legible if they are simply committed to them. Audiences don't want to be taught a dictionary—they want to be invited into a living conversation. When you stage the crowd as a character, the vernacular becomes part of the drama: the audience learns it the way any character in a play would—by watching, by listening, by being present in the moment.

Directing Moments of Connection

One of the deepest, often unspoken expectations in a concert audience is the desire for personal validation from the artist. Every fan, on some level, hopes to be seen—to make eye contact, to be waved at, to get a shout-out. Of course, this is logistically impossible. No artist can personally acknowledge every individual in a crowd of thousands. But a well-directed show understands this and builds in moments that simulate connection in strategic, theatrical ways. One of the most effective and time-tested techniques is the use of what might be called a symbolic audience surrogate—a plant, or at least a moment of recognition, given to a visibly "deserving" attendee.

Take Wayne Newton, for example. In the cheesiest but most effective of gestures, he would find someone in a wheelchair at his Las Vegas shows, walk off the stage, hold their hand, and sing directly to them. And the rest of the audience didn't feel left out—instead, they felt emotionally satisfied. They accepted that this person was more worthy of the artist's attention, and in seeing that moment, they experienced a kind of collective validation. It's a shorthand, a theatrical trick, but a powerful one. And it also addresses a deeper truth: if everyone is made to feel special, then no one really is. Authentic connection must be selective to feel real. The director's job is to create the illusion of intimacy—carefully, intentionally—so that the audience feels seen, even if only through someone else.

Here's the basic mechanics of how to do this.

In the old days of Las Vegas, when people bought tickets by phone or in person, the box office would routinely ask, "Are you celebrating a special occasion?" That simple question became one of the most useful tools in the performer's arsenal. It created a ready-made profile of the audience, complete with seat locations. Armed with that knowledge, Wayne Newton—or any headliner of the era—could build a moment into the show where he'd say, "We have someone very special with us tonight. [Guest Name] is celebrating a [special occasion]." It was a small gesture, but it carried enormous weight, because it transformed anonymous ticket holders into part of the story.

Today, social media makes this even easier. A quick scan of fan accounts and public posts before the show reveals who is celebrating a birthday, a graduation, an anniversary, or something even more significant. That information can be woven directly into the performance. The hierarchy is straightforward: if there is a medical recovery, a surgery, or any life-altering challenge, choose that first. Then work your way down through rarer milestones toward the most common—birthdays being the bottom of the ladder. These are the people you highlight during the show.

The key, however, is restraint. If you call out too many audience members, the moment stops feeling special. Everyone starts waiting to hear their name announced between songs, and the effect becomes transactional. Once per show is enough. Done sparingly, it feels like a gift; done repeatedly, it feels like a raffle.

When you do choose to spotlight someone, it's not enough to say, "I know you exist." You must go a step further, but not too far. The sweet spot is just enough detail to show you care, without crossing into the uncanny territory of sounding like you've stalked their personal life. Then, frame that recognition with something motivational—link their story to the band's story, or to the shared spirit of the evening.

For example: "We have someone very special with us tonight—Sara Smith. Where are you, Sara? Sara was in a bad car accident last month. She lost her job because she couldn't walk, and now she's better. She bought these tickets six months ago, and we are so grateful she's here with us tonight. You know, our drummer's cousin went through a similar accident last year, and we all took turns sitting with them in the hospital, not knowing what the future would hold. So thank you, Sara, for letting us share this night with you—and thank all of you for being here to spend it together."

On a larger scale, the same principle can be staged with even more spectacle. Lady Gaga, for instance, used to call someone sitting in the balcony on her tour's sponsored cell phone. Cameras would cut to that fan as they answered, and Gaga would tell them directly, "I called to let you know you're special." The rest of the audience didn't feel excluded—they felt included in the drama of witnessing someone like them being chosen.

George Strait took the idea further, using a portion of ticket sales to buy a house for a veteran in the armed services. At a carefully staged moment in the show, he would bring that veteran onstage and announce that everyone in the arena had helped pay for their new home. The entire audience experienced the validation, because it was framed as a collective act of generosity.

The scale can be adjusted to fit the venue. In an arena, it's a house. In a theater, it might be a phone call. In a nightclub, it might be as simple as knowing someone had posted about getting an $80 parking ticket last week—and then surprising them mid-show with $80 cash, explaining that the audience's ticket money had "covered" their fine. The size of the gesture doesn't matter. What matters is that it feels personal, theatrical, and rooted in the shared presence of everyone in the room.

That is the structure: recognition, context, connection, gratitude. If you can build that into a single moment of the show, the entire audience will feel as though they've been seen, because they've witnessed one of their own being lifted up.

But when you build a moment of recognition into the show, you also have to confront the uncomfortable reality of what I call the regulars—the small group of repeat attendees who believe that showing up multiple nights in a row entitles them to a starring role. These are the people who arrive armed with giant signs that block the view of everyone behind them, or who hover at the edge of the barricade angling for attention as if the show were a customer-service desk. And at the extreme end, you get the ones who bring small children to every date of the tour, hoisting them into the air in the hope that the artist will bring the child onstage.

Some of these parents will repeat this behavior a dozen times, treating the performance as an audition for their kid. If you watch their faces, especially during the moment the child goes up in the air, you see something brittle and desperate that the audience around them picks up on instantly. It repels people who are there for one night, who saved money and made plans and simply want to enjoy the show. Their experience is quietly spoiled by someone else's entitlement. As director, you must account for this when crafting the validation moment—placing it where it can be controlled, shaped, and insulated from the people who try to commandeer it. The goal is to give the audience a gift, not to reward the most aggressive bidder.

You should discuss this with the artist, their manager, and the tour manager (if they've worked with this artist before) about this issue. If it's a known problem then there will also be times when, for security or logistical reasons, you'll need to use a plant. That's a legitimate tool, but in the age of social media it comes with risks. The same "fan" appearing at multiple shows with the same story will be exposed within hours, and what was meant as a gift quickly curdles into a con. If you use plants, make sure it's a different person with a different story every night. Authenticity—or at least the appearance of it—is non-negotiable. The moment the audience feels tricked, they stop feeling rewarded and start feeling cheated.

Creating Participatory Rituals and Call-and-Response

One of the clearest signs that a show is not meeting the emotional needs of its audience is when people begin shouting at the artist mid-performance. Whether it's a song request, a profession of love, or a boast about having driven six hours to be there, what those outbursts signal is a craving for personal validation that the show has failed to satisfy.

These interruptions don't happen in a vacuum—they happen because the audience feels emotionally neglected, or uncertain of their place in the experience. They're reaching out, loudly, because they want to be pulled in. As a director, your job is to anticipate and neutralize that impulse—not by scolding it, but by designing a show that satiates it before it erupts. You know you've done your job well when no one feels the need to yell. When the emotional pacing is clear, when the artist's presence feels intimate even from a distance, and when moments of connection are built into the flow of the performance, the audience will stay engaged and quiet. Not because they're bored—but because they're fulfilled. Silence, in this context, is not a lack of energy. It's evidence that the show is working.

The most effective way to redirect that craving for attention is to give the audience structured outlets for participation. Humans want to be involved, but they also want guidance. If you don't provide it, they'll invent their own ways of inserting themselves into the show—usually in ways that break immersion. If you do provide it, they'll embrace it gratefully, because it channels their energy into something that feels both communal and sanctioned.

This is where participatory rituals come in. Call-and-response, choreographed gestures, repeated chants—these are not filler, they are pressure valves. They create moments where the audience gets to feel heard without hijacking the flow of the performance. Done well, these rituals evolve into traditions. Fans expect them, newcomers learn them by imitation, and the artist no longer has to beg for participation—it happens automatically.

Think about James Brown barking a line only to have the band and audience shout it back. Or Freddie Mercury at Live Aid, teasing the crowd with a simple vocal riff that 50,000 people echoed back in perfect rhythm. Neither of those moments was accidental. They were carefully rehearsed, placed at points in the set where energy needed to crest and release. The artistry wasn't just in the music—it was in the timing of when the audience was invited to become part of the band.

The director's task is to map out these rituals with the same precision as lighting cues or scene changes. What words or sounds are easy enough to mimic that 10,000 people can do it in unison? How long can you sustain the exchange before it drags? Where in the setlist does it amplify momentum, and where would it stall it? Participation only works when it feels like a natural extension of the show's rhythm. Misplace it, and it becomes awkward. Place it correctly, and it transforms a crowd into a chorus.

A couple of things to look out for with call-and-response: it should never be complicated. The moment the audience has to think too hard, the energy drops. Forget the cliché of, "Everyone on the left say yeah, everyone on the right say no." It's clumsy, it divides the room, and it forces people into a drill-sergeant exercise instead of a shared ritual.

Keep it simple—simple enough that a toddler could do it. If words need to be shouted back, they should be words that can be shouted clearly even with a mouth full of food. Short, percussive syllables win over long phrases every time. And the best call-and-response is built on imitation, not explanation. When the performer sings a phrase, the audience instinctively echoes it. No instructions, no preamble—just a reflex. That way, the crowd doesn't feel like they're following orders. They feel like they're part of a game they already know how to play.

The deeper truth is this: call-and-response is not about volume, it's about belonging. When the audience shouts something back in unison, what they're really saying is, "We are part of this." They no longer feel neglected, so the urge to interrupt disappears. They have been woven into the story. And once that bond is formed, it carries through the entire night.

Chapter 11
Dialogue and Banter
What to Say When the Song Ends

Why "Hello Cleveland!" Isn't Enough

The moment the house lights drop and the first chord rings out, adrenaline floods the stage. Performers are wired, hearts hammering, bodies buzzing. And in that surge, they reach for the easiest release valve they know: the microphone. Out comes the primal yell—"Hello Cleveland!"—or its countless variations. Sometimes it's the city's name, screamed like a touchdown cheer. Sometimes it's the suburbs, reeled off like a weather report: "We've got anyone here tonight from Shaker Heights? Bay Village? Westlake?" Other times it's whatever headline was on their phone two hours ago, or worse, a sudden detour into politics when the rest of the show has nothing to do with politics at all.

These bursts feel natural in the moment. They feel alive. The performer believes they are connecting. But from the audience's perspective, more often than not, it's static. It interrupts the arc you've built. It fractures the illusion. The show was carrying them into a world—musical, visual, emotional—and then suddenly they're yanked back into the present tense, into today's news cycle, into a geography lesson, into a soapbox rant. Theatrical energy collapses into everyday chatter.

The core problem isn't malice; it's chemistry. Adrenaline is not a writer. It has no sense of pacing or tone. A performer high on adrenaline believes their every thought is golden, their every impulse profound. But adrenaline makes you louder, not smarter. What feels like revelation in the moment often reads as noise to the audience. Banter

DOI: 10.4324/9781003679332-11

delivered this way is like an unscored drum fill—it may feel satisfying to the drummer, but it disrupts the song.

Improvised chatter has another hidden cost: it is almost never in the same emotional key as the material surrounding it. Imagine a show that has been carefully staged to lead into a ballad of heartbreak and loss. The lights dim, the screens fall quiet, the band softens to a hush—and then the singer, riding their adrenaline high, bellows, "How's everybody doing tonight?!" The tension evaporates. The world collapses. The ballad hasn't even started, and already the audience has been shoved out of the story.

This is why "Hello Cleveland" isn't enough. A concert isn't a pep rally. It isn't a press conference. It's a story told through music, light, movement, costume, and atmosphere. Every word spoken into the microphone is part of that story, whether the performer realizes it or not. And when those words are improvised without intention, they betray the very thing the show has been building: coherence.

The mistake most performers make is assuming that the audience wants to hear their raw, unfiltered, in-the-moment thoughts. But that's not why people paid for a ticket. If the crowd wanted off-the-cuff chatter, they could watch a livestream from the artist's kitchen. What they came for is the world of the show—the heightened, intentional reality you've constructed.

That means the banter between songs isn't a break from the world. It's a part of it. The audience wants to feel that every word spoken to them is of the same fabric as the lighting, the costumes, the setlist. They want it to feel inevitable, not improvised. When the singer leans into the mic and says something between songs, the best reaction in the house is not, "Oh, that's what they happened to be thinking tonight." It's, "Of course they would say that here. That's exactly what belongs in this moment."

Think about it this way: if the songs are the dialogue of the play, then the banter is the stage whisper to the audience. It's not meant to shatter the illusion; it's meant to deepen it. The crowd wants to feel like they are part of the conversation already unfolding inside the show's universe. A casual phrase, a repeated ritual, even a joke told night after night—all of it can feel intimate if it grows out of the same soil as the rest of the performance.

The great performers understand this instinctively. They don't step out of character to chat with the audience; they pull the audience into the character's orbit. They make the crowd feel as though they've been invited into a private world, one where even the throwaway asides belong. Done well, banter doesn't feel like an interruption. It feels like a secret being shared—a reminder that the thousands of people in the room are not spectators, but participants in the same imagined reality.

Take KISS as the simplest illustration of why "Hello Cleveland" doesn't serve the show. They walk onstage in kabuki makeup and monster costumes, fireballs exploding, lasers cutting across the arena. The conceit is clear: we are not in an arena anymore—we are in KISS world, some intergalactic fantasy where demons and star children and cat men shred guitars in zero gravity. And then, the lead singer bellows into the mic: "Hello, Cleveland!" Instantly the illusion cracks. How does a spaceman from outer space know what Cleveland is? Cleveland doesn't exist in this world. By dragging the audience back to geography, the spell collapses. For two minutes we believed in the myth; with one phrase, we're reminded we're in a hockey arena in Ohio. That's why "Hello Cleveland" doesn't just fall flat—it actively punctures the world the show worked so hard to build.

Another banter cliché just as deadly is the stock phrase: "We're going to play some new songs and some old songs." It sounds harmless, but what does it actually mean? Nothing. Every band since the dawn of touring has played some new songs and some old songs. It's not information; it's filler. Worse, it tells the audience that the performer has stepped out of the world of the show and into the role of a salesman, announcing product categories instead of sustaining the illusion. The second you draw attention to the machinery of the setlist, the magic thins. The audience isn't waiting for a balance sheet of new versus old—they want to feel that each song is arriving because this is the only possible next step in the story you're telling. Reducing it to "new ones and old ones" breaks that spell, flattening narrative into bookkeeping.

And if you are touring a show built around hits from a past decade, resist the urge to ask, "Who remembers the 1970s?" or "Who remembers the 1980s?" On paper, it sounds like a nostalgic wink. In practice, it's a blunt reminder of age, mortality, and the fact that time has passed since those songs were new. Instead of making the audience feel included, it makes them feel old—or worse, excluded if they weren't alive in that decade. The songs themselves already carry the weight of memory. Let them do the work. Asking who "remembers" turns a living performance into a museum piece, and the show collapses into self-conscious nostalgia rather than timeless immediacy.

Writing or Improvising Meaningful Stage Dialogue

Stage dialogue should never be filler. It is not wallpaper between songs. It is part of the architecture of the night, as deliberate as the lighting cue or the costume change. The words a performer speaks on stage should inspire, provoke, or prepare the audience for the emotional terrain they are about to enter. Even a single sentence can function as a doorway: the right words pull the audience across the threshold, ready to receive what comes next.

But what happens when your performers aren't natural talkers? Not every artist is a born raconteur. Many bar bands simply don't have much to say. Some singers are uncomfortable speaking at all, terrified of breaking the musical spell with their own voices. Others fall back on the tired cliché: "Is everybody having a good time tonight?"—which is really no question at all, since the audience has no choice but to shout "yes."

There is a simple, almost foolproof alternative: give the performer a book of poetry. Twice in a set, maybe three times if it feels right, have them open the book, select a piece that resonates with the mood of the scene, and simply read it aloud. It doesn't have to be their writing. It doesn't have to be famous. It just has to align with the world of the show. A love poem before a ballad of heartbreak. A fragment of haiku before a song about stillness. A raw, jagged verse before a wall of distortion.

The act of reading poetry from a physical book instantly reframes the stage. It slows time, forces the audience to lean in, and communicates that something intentional is happening. Suddenly, the band that seemed like a bar band a moment ago feels like they are reaching for something larger. The words don't need to be complex—the act itself is the message: this show is about more than noise; it is about meaning. Poetry is just one example. Imagine the dissonance created by a band where the bass player starts reading a couple of pages of "The Cat in the Hat" between songs, progressively finishing the story over the course of the show. And in that moment, the audience pays sharper attention to what follows, because the performer has invited them into a ritual rather than a routine.

It almost doesn't matter what the words are, so long as they provoke the right feeling. The audience isn't parsing the literal meaning of every syllable—they are tuning into tone, rhythm, and emotional suggestion. If the goal is to prepare them for melancholy, then the words could come from a sonnet, a horoscope, or even a debit card statement read with the weight of confession. If the goal is to spark energy, the performer could recite advertisements like incantations. Context transforms content. What matters is not the source of the text but the emotional resonance it sets into motion. That is how you create what the audience experiences as meaningful stage dialogue: not by finding the perfect sentence, but by shaping the atmosphere so that any sentence lands like prophecy.

Imagine this in practice: the band finishes a song, the last chord hangs in the air, and instead of the front person trotting out the empty script—"Thanks for coming out tonight, hope you're having fun"—they open their mouth and begin to read a list of random words. Slowly. Deliberately. Apple. Window. Silence. Breath. Stone. Each word lands in the pause before the next. The audience leans in, wondering what it means, and then the next song begins. Nothing profound has been said, but the moment feels charged, uncanny, ritualistic. Already, it is a million times more powerful than the reflexive patter of small talk. It signals that everything spoken on this stage has purpose, even when it doesn't make sense. And that alone is enough to keep the audience leaning forward, believing.

Structuring Talking Moments to Serve the Show

Talking moments work best when they fall into the natural breathing spaces of the night. Not every song needs a spoken bridge, and not every silence needs to be filled. Look at your setlist as a map: where are the peaks, where are the valleys, where are the transitions? A well-placed sentence before a shift in tone can prepare the audience emotionally for what comes next. A ritual phrase before a band's biggest hit can elevate the anticipation rather than kill it with overexplanation.

You should also look carefully at the practical transitions in the set—the dead air moments that audiences usually endure. If you know the guitarist has to swap instruments, or the drummer needs to adjust hardware, or a laptop needs to load the next sequence, that is a perfect spot for dialogue. Instead of awkward silence and visible tinkering, the performer's words cover the gap, turning downtime into design. By overlapping banter with logistical necessities, you preserve momentum, hide the mechanics, and make the audience believe the pause was always part of the show.

We also want to prepare banter for technical problems. Something will go wrong. A cable fails, a string snaps, a laptop freezes, the lights die. Panic makes most performers ramble, apologize, or worse—break the illusion by acknowledging the machinery. Instead, give them a handful of prepared phrases or rituals they can lean on when the show stumbles. It could be a short joke that always fits their persona, a verse they can repeat until the problem is solved, or even silence that feels intentional because it has been rehearsed. Think of it as emotional insurance: when disaster strikes, the performer doesn't have to invent—they just reach for the prepared tool, and the world of the show stays intact.

Or this could be the perfect moment to break out the book of poetry. A brief reading can transform a technical delay from a flaw into a feature. Whatever the strategy, the point is the same: be prepared for what to say when it happens. A rehearsed response turns an accident into part of the show, keeping the audience inside the world instead of watching the machinery creak.

In fact, the smartest preparation is to have one line ready for every song in the set where things might break. That way, no matter where the train derails, the performer has an emotional rope to pull the audience back on board. If the glitch happens before the ballad, they have a phrase that deepens the hush instead of shattering it. If it happens before the anthem, they have a line that fuels anticipation instead of draining it. These are not generic apologies; they are scene-specific bridges, crafted to keep the mood alive. One prepared sentence per song is enough. When the inevitable happens, the performer doesn't scramble—they already know exactly what to say to rethread the world and carry everyone forward.

Beyond broken equipment, the live environment will always surprise you. A drunk heckler. A fight in the pit. A fire alarm. A celebrity walking in. These moments can either derail the night or become part of its mythology. If you want them to serve the show, you must prepare performers with flexible, in-character responses. The line doesn't have to be specific—it just has to belong to the world you've built. A demon can acknowledge a heckler differently than a folk singer. A glam icon can turn a security interruption into part of the pageant. The unforeseen doesn't have to be an interruption; it can be absorbed into the story, provided you've thought about who your performers are and how their onstage selves would respond.

Stage dialogue is not an afterthought—it is part of the show's architecture, as essential as light, costume, or sound. The words between songs either reinforce the world you've built or puncture it, and the difference comes down to intention. Whether it's a carefully scripted ritual, a line prepared for a breakdown, or a poem read aloud in silence, the goal is always the same: keep the audience inside the world. If you treat banter as part of the score rather than a distraction from it, every word becomes another instrument, shaping the rhythm of the night and carrying the crowd deeper into the story you want them to believe.

Chapter 12
Special Guests, Features, and Surprises

Managing Drop-Ins and Short-Run Guests

Before you choreograph a single entrance, before you assign a single lighting cue, before you even allow yourself to imagine the applause that will erupt the moment the surprise guest steps into the frame, you have one job: figure out why this person is here.

Not what they will perform, not how they will walk on, not whether the audience will scream, cry, or faint.

Why.
Because until you understand the purpose of the cameo, every artistic decision you make is a shot in the dark.

There are only three reasons a guest appears in a show, and each one creates a completely different artistic reality:

The guest is endorsing your artist.
This is the “blessing from above” model. A legend, an icon, a senior figure, or someone with cultural gravity steps into your world for a moment. Their presence acts as a stamp of approval. In this scenario, the power flows from the guest downward: their appearance elevates your artist. That hierarchy dictates everything—framing, staging, lighting, billing, even where the bodies stand.

Your artist is endorsing the guest.
This is the “platform boost” model. The guest is rising, emerging, or simply less known to the audience. Your artist is lending credibility,

DOI: 10.4324/9781003679332-12

visibility, and story. The power flows in the opposite direction. The cameo becomes an act of generosity, mentorship, or spotlight-sharing. The staging must reflect that: your artist becomes the host, not the beneficiary.

The cameo is happening for personal or vanity reasons.

Maybe the headliner is obsessed with this person. Maybe they grew up idolizing them. Maybe they've always dreamed of performing together. Maybe a manager pushed it through because two people hit it off at an awards show afterparty. Fine. Vanity is a real factor in touring. But even vanity needs dramaturgy.

Because no matter the backstage reason, the audience still sees a power exchange. So you must decide—explicitly, artistically—what direction that power is moving in. Is the guest endorsing the artist? Is the artist endorsing the guest? Or is this a mutual exchange, a meeting of equals?

There is no such thing as a neutral cameo. Someone is always lending status to someone else, and if you don't choose which way that current flows, the moment will choose for you—often badly. When audiences sense confusion in power dynamics, the cameo reads as awkward, desperate, or random. When the hierarchy is clear, even the smallest interaction becomes meaningful.

You also need to design three distinct versions of the cameo—one for each endorsement dynamic—because the staging, framing, and emotional temperature change completely depending on who is giving power to whom. The "guest-endorses-artist" version centers your performer as the gravitational body, with the guest entering as a deliberate beam of validation. The "artist-endorses-guest" version flips that, requiring the headliner to create space, offer focus, and literally reposition themselves to spotlight the visitor. And the mutual-endorsement version must be staged like a convergence: two worlds meeting at a single point, neither outranking the other, with blocking that emphasizes equality rather than hierarchy. If you build only one version, you will be unprepared for the reality that endorsement dynamics shift nightly—based on the city, the guest's fame level, the audience's demographics, or simply the chemistry between the performers. Three versions ensure you can choose the one that tells the truth of this performance, in this venue, with this guest, instead of forcing every cameo into the same rigid template.

And, of course, there's the wildcard option: throw all of that out the window and design a cameo slot that isn't tied to music, hierarchy, or even a specific person. A modular cameo—like the Lady Gaga example I referenced earlier—functions as a narrative beat rather than a duet. It can be filled by a fan, a plant, a local figure, or a celebrity without breaking the show's logic because the moment isn't about the guest's identity; it's about the action they perform. This kind of cameo is structurally liberating: instead of calibrating status, you're designing a ritual. A repeatable beat with flexible casting. The tension isn't "Who showed up?" but "How will tonight's person embody this moment?" When you design the cameo as a task rather than a collaboration, you free the show from dependency on fame levels, scheduling, or power dynamics—and create a nightly surprise that remains cohesive no matter who steps into it (more recent examples of this role can be found in the Charli XCX "Apple Dance" cameo or the Sabrina Carpenter "Onstage Arrest" cameo).

Planning Cameos for Maximum Effect

If you're not using the nightly non-musical cameo—and you're committing to a true musical cameo—then you have to confront an uncomfortable truth: musical cameos are landmines. They sound glamorous, they look great on paper, and they make for excellent social media clips, but in terms of narrative integrity they are one of the fastest ways to detonate the emotional architecture you've spent hours, days, or months constructing.

The problem begins the moment the headliner performs a song by the guest artist. On stage it feels generous, collaborative, celebratory. But to the audience, it scrambles the signal. They came to your show. They're orienting themselves around your emotional world, your vocabulary, your sound. The instant you pivot into a cover simply because tonight's special guest wrote it, you introduce a new gravitational center the audience was never prepared for. Suddenly they're wondering, "Wait—whose concert is this? Why are we here? What story am I following?" You've cracked the frame of the world, and once cracked, it's hard to restore.

The inverse is just as damaging. If your guest arrives to sing your song—but the purpose of the cameo is to elevate the guest—the power dynamics misalign. Instead of boosting their status, the arrangement inadvertently spotlights how dependent they are on you to even appear. The audience senses that imbalance immediately and the cameo stops feeling like an endorsement and starts feeling like a pity feature. Worse, it muddies the emotional meaning of the song itself. A song that was built to be intimate becomes cluttered by a new presence that doesn't belong there dramatically.

This is why, whenever possible, you should resist the instinct to make a cameo musical at all. Non-musical cameos preserve the narrative arc. They slip in and out of the show without threatening the emotional spine. But if you absolutely must create a musical cameo, its safest placement is outside the body of the show—either before the narrative begins (as a pre-show moment, a warmup, an opening number, or even a surprise opener) or after the story has concluded (as an encore, tag, curtain-call event, or post-show celebration). Framing the cameo as an external bonus rather than an internal chapter allows the audience to enjoy it without recalibrating their understanding of the concert's world. You protect your emotional arc, you protect your pacing, and you still get the thrill of the special guest—without sacrificing the integrity of the show you've built.

Avoiding Awkward Transitions

The first thing you must lock down—before blocking, before lighting, before the guest even rehearses—is where this character is coming from and where they are going to. This is why the endorsement logic mattered so much in the previous section: you cannot stage a clean transition unless you first understand the cameo's narrative purpose. A guest doesn't simply "appear." They arrive from somewhere, and they leave to somewhere, and the psychological and emotional tone of those two imaginary locations shapes the entire moment.

This matters because the most dangerous part of any cameo is the entrance. The second the guest walks onstage, the audience's emotional compass spins wildly. Some will erupt with joy, some will scream so loudly they forget what song they're in, and some may have a complicated or even negative relationship with the guest. All of that emotional noise floods the room at once. The cameo becomes a rupture—unless you have already built a narrative bridge to carry the audience across it.

So you must decide:

Did the guest just step out of a limousine and rush in with glamorous urgency?
Did they fly in from another city just for this one moment?
Are they a local friend who came straight from home?
Are they pretending they just happened to wander by the theater and couldn't resist joining the show?
Are they framed as a mythic figure who materializes only when summoned?
Or are they a casual human visitor slipping into the world for a brief, private exchange?

Whatever the fiction is, it must be specific, because the fiction dictates the behavior. The guest's entrance and exit are performances in themselves. How they walk, how fast they move, whether their body carries purpose or hesitation, whether they appear grounded or electrified—every detail signals to the audience what kind of interruption this is supposed to be. And if you fail to define it, the audience will create their own explanation—which is almost always messier and more chaotic than the one you would have built.

Ideally, the cameo should feel dreamlike: a figure who emerges out of nowhere and dissolves just as quickly. In and out. A visitation rather than a detour. The reason this works is simple: dream logic prevents the audience from having to renegotiate the rules of the world. The moment arrives, illuminates the sky, and disappears, leaving no footprint on the narrative path. It is only when the entrance becomes a spectacle—when the guest is introduced like a conquering hero, when the headliner milks the applause—that the spell breaks. The fanfare gratifies the performers, but destabilizes the show.

This is why defining the "from" and the "to" is essential. It allows you to choreograph the entry as a clean insertion into the world rather than a derailment, and to choreograph the exit as a vanishing—quiet, efficient, and narratively respectful. When the guest arrives with intention and leaves with intention, the audience stays inside the story. When they arrive with fanfare and leave with chaos, the audience forgets what story they were in to begin with.

Transitions succeed when they feel invisible.

They fail when they feel celebrated.

Your job is to make the cameo feel like a breath of wind—present, undeniable, but never disruptive to the weather of the world you've built.

Chapter 13
Designing for the Road
Portability and Scale

Modular Set Design

Modular design begins long before the set designer starts sketching. It begins in a parking lot.

You are not the tour manager, and you are not the set designer, but this is the point in the process where the two must work together—along with the artists—under one clear framework. On most tours at the club and theater level, the performers are not just performers. They are part of the load-in crew, the load-out crew, and the overnight-hauling-the-van crew. That reality shapes every creative choice. Ignore it and the tour will punish you for your imagination.

Before anyone builds a single scenic element, you need to know exactly how much physical space the show occupies when it is packed. Not hypothetically. Not "roughly." Exactly. The only way to discover that is to rehearse it.

Rent the vehicle you will tour in—van, bus, or truck—and secure a parking lot for a full day. Bring the band and every crew member who will touch gear. Then load the vehicle with only the equipment required to perform the show. No "maybe we'll need it," no personal extras, no sentimental clutter. Strip the show to its functional core and load only that. Once everything essential is inside, you will immediately see how much room remains for merchandise and how much room remains for your set. Those leftover inches form the boundary within which the set designer must work.

This boundary is not a creative limitation; it is the foundation of modular design. A modular set is defined not by how cleverly it unfolds

DOI: 10.4324/9781003679332-13

onstage, but by how efficiently it moves from venue to vehicle and back again. The set must be built to the exact physical truth you discovered in the parking lot. Anything larger becomes dead weight. Anything fragile becomes a liability.

Once the designer has created pieces that honor those constraints, you repeat the process. Rent the vehicle again. Return to the same parking lot. Load and unload the show with the actual scenic elements. This second rehearsal exposes the problems that only appear when people are tired, the sun is setting, and the last case refuses to clear the door by two inches. You fix those problems here, not at midnight behind a club in Kansas City.

Think of the scene in the Michael Keaton film *The Founder* where the McDonald brothers chalk out their entire kitchen on the ground and rehearse the movement of a hamburger line before a single counter is built. They test the system physically, not conceptually. They eliminate inefficiency until the operation runs without friction. That is the same thing you are doing, you are choreographing the movement of the show before the set exists onstage.

This is modular design: a system built from hard limits, physical rehearsal, and repeatable efficiency. A set that loads well will tour well. A set that tours well will perform consistently. Consistency is the director's ally. Everything else is decoration.

Adapting to Different Venue Sizes and Shapes

Every touring show, whether it admits it or not, is designed for one stage size—the ideal one. The trick is making the ideal flexible. The goal is simple: build a show that fits a slightly larger stage than you usually get, and then design it so it can contract without breaking. Expanding a show is easy; compressing it exposes every weakness in the structure. If the set only works when it breathes fully, then it's a set designed for a photograph, not a tour.

Sometimes, though, the geometry refuses to cooperate. A club with a postage-stamp stage one night, a festival with a hangar-sized deck the next, a black box theater the night after that. When the shapes are radically incompatible, you are no longer scaling—you are switching worlds. In those cases, the only honest solution is to build two versions of the show and bring both with you. This used to be unrealistic unless you were touring with corporate money or full-time trucks. Today, with lighter materials, collapsible structures, and digital assets replacing part of the physical burden, running dual versions is often not just possible but practical. The real question is whether you designed for that possibility from the beginning.

The way you achieve this flexibility is not through complexity—it's through simple geometry. The strongest touring shows are built from basic shapes: squares, circles, and triangles, repeated physically and spatially. And always remember: the stage itself is a rectangle, whether it's a proscenium, a club deck, or a festival platform. Everything you build has to live inside that rectangular frame. Your squares, circles, and triangles must fit within that box in a way that still tells the same story at every scale. A square can become a platform, a wall, a riser, or a boundary. A circle can be a drum layout, a lighting halo, or a staging perimeter. A triangle can be a ramp, a brace, a directional force. These shapes scale cleanly. They compress without distortion. They rearrange themselves logically in both large and small spaces because they begin as simple forms designed to fit inside a rigid outline.

When you design environments using these shapes—rather than elaborate one-off constructions—you create a vocabulary the crew can manipulate in real time. The show becomes modular not just inside the van but on the stage itself. A square that sits 12 feet upstage in a theater can sit four feet downstage in a club. A triangular brace that frames a singer in a wide proscenium can flip sideways and become a dividing line in a cramped bar. The shapes don't care where they live. They simply adapt.

This isn't mathematical minimalism for its own sake; it's a survival strategy. A touring show that relies on odd angles, bespoke curves, or one exact footprint is a show built for disappointment. A show built on primary shapes, used intentionally and consistently, becomes elastic. And elasticity is what keeps the show coherent no matter where it lands.

Your task, as the director, is to treat scale changes not as disasters but as part of the design language. The audience does not care whether the deck is 30 feet wide or 15. They care whether the world feels deliberate. A show that contracts cleanly feels intentional. A show that collapses haphazardly feels compromised.

Build the world from shapes that scale. Treat each venue size as a variation, not a setback. And if the tour truly demands two different shows, embrace it without embarrassment. Consistency is not about sameness—it's about clarity. A clear world is one that can survive any stage it encounters.

The Art of Compromise without Losing Vision

By now you've already faced the truth that touring is a negotiation. You build a world, and the world pushes back. Venues with architectural features you didn't ask for. Crew members who prioritize functionality over aesthetics. Festival environments where half the stage picture is competing with a beer tent, an LED sponsor wall, or a Ferris wheel. You can't control all of it. Some nights you can barely control half of it. But a touring show doesn't survive because every condition is perfect; it survives because its foundation is strong enough to keep its identity intact under pressure.

A clear show communicates even when the environment is working against it. That clarity comes from structure, not spectacle. If the world you built has a spine—visual, emotional, and practical—it will carry its message no matter how compromised the frame becomes. The audience may not receive the version you imagined, but they will receive the version that matters.

This is where compromise becomes a craft rather than a defeat. At this stage in the process, you should identify the elements of your show that feel non-negotiable. Not preferences. Not luxuries. The actual structural load-bearing components: the sightlines a key moment depends on, the lighting cue that defines a shift in emotional temperature, the physical spatial relationship that anchors a performer's presence. Write them down. Be ruthless about how few they should be.

Once you have that list, your job is to make each item negotiable in extreme circumstances without destroying the integrity of the work. That may sound contradictory, but it's the director's paradox: you protect the core by accepting reality in advance and designing the escape routes before you need them. If you know that an unavoidable truss position will block your lighting cue in a certain venue, you plan the alternate configuration now. If you know a festival will restrict your ability to control the background, you design a version of the moment that shifts focus inward rather than outward. If you know that a stage feature will pull attention away from the performer, you prepare a countercomposition that redirects the audience's eye.

This isn't surrender. It's strategy. A director who refuses to bend ends up breaking their own show. A director who plans for compromise ensures that compromise never becomes erosion.

The key is that every adjustment must still express the same underlying intention. You are not designing multiple shows; you are designing one show with multiple paths to the same emotional destination. If the foundation is solid—if the geometry is sound, if the story is clear, if the physical world has integrity—then the show will read no matter how much the surroundings attempt to dilute it. The audience won't know what changed. They'll only know what they felt.

You can't control every building, every festival, or every crew. But you can control the strength of your own design. And a strong design is one that knows exactly what it must protect—and how it will protect it—long before the first truck door rolls open.

Chapter 14
The Rehearsal Process
Making the Most of Limited Time

Designing a Show that Fits within Real-World Time Constraints

If every chapter up to now has been about shaping the inner world of the concert—the story, the imagery, the staging—this one is about the clock. The literal clock. The one mounted backstage, above the monitor desk, silently judging you. Because for all our romantic talk about emotional arcs and immersive worlds, the truth is blunt: your show lives or dies by time. Not theatrical time. Not emotional time. Actual, contractual, union-enforced, financially binding time. Touring isn't poetry. It's labor law. And if you forget that, even for one night, the consequences are immediate and brutal.

Curfew is not a suggestion; it's the cost of doing business. Most cities, venues, and union contracts come with strictly defined work hours, and when the clock flips to the cutoff, everything after that becomes overtime. For major union houses—stagehands, riggers, electricians—violating curfew can wipe out the entire night's profit in minutes. Run ten minutes long and you may already be paying time-and-a-half. Drift into the next hour and you could be in double-time. Push further and some locals escalate to golden time, which is triple pay, applied across multiple departments simultaneously. Multiply that by dozens of crew members and then multiply again by the departments classified as essential personnel. You can easily burn the merch profit, the door profit, the promoter cut, and possibly the artist's guaranteed fee. On a truly bad night, you can put the show into debt. The audience may see

DOI: 10.4324/9781003679332-14

thousands of people in the building, but behind the scenes you're losing money because a ballad stretched too long. It is preventable, and it is your responsibility.

One of the tried-and-true ways of dealing with this problem is to have some kind of clock visible to the performers, but more often than not, the clock ends up being visible to the audience in some way. Either it's an LED display shining onstage, awkwardly out of place in the wings, or the performer looks at it in a way that breaks character. Part of building the world of your show is finding a way to hide the clock—and to conceal how the performer becomes aware of real-world time.

This is why every set you design has to be time-literate. When you build the setlist, shape transitions, rehearse choreography, develop staging ideas, or write cues, you must know to the minute how long each section runs. Not approximately. Not "usually about." Exactly. That means clocking run-throughs in rehearsal, timing transitions with the crew exactly as they will unfold live, tracking every second of dead air such as applause, tuning, banter, or water breaks, and paying attention to historical drift points where performers tend to lose track of time. You need to understand variable elements like extended solos, guest features, or audience interactions, and you need to hold a clear estimate of all of them together. Only then can you understand the true shape of the night and how likely it is to drift.

The part no one warns you about is the opposite problem: you also cannot finish too early. Promoters often specify a minimum performance length. Sometimes it is 75 minutes, sometimes 90, sometimes a full two hours. Ending short can put you in breach of contract. That can mean fines, lost bonuses, or a damaged relationship with the promoter who hired you. So the director's paradox becomes clear: you cannot run long and you cannot run short. You must land the plane at the exact minute the contract demands.

To make that possible, you need two invisible systems in place. The first is what I call the stretch kit, which is a set of moments within the show that can expand naturally if necessary. These might take the form of a story the artist can tell, an outro the band can loop for a little longer, a call-and-response section that breathes, an acoustic verse that can be added, or an extra chorus the lighting team can trigger without breaking the world of the show. These moments must be woven into the design of the performance so that lengthening them feels like an organic part of the emotional arc, not a last-minute scramble to fill space.

The second system is the parachute, the opposite of the stretch kit, meant for nights when the show begins to drift too long. This might be a trimmed intro, a bridge removed from a mid-set song, a shortened bit of banter, a B-side cut entirely, or a transition collapsed into a hard blackout. The important part is that none of these decisions are improvised in real time. They are rehearsed versions of the show, known and understood by the performers, the stage manager, the lighting and sound departments, the camera operators, and anyone else whose cues or actions are tied to the sequence of events. You're not saving the night through chaos. You're executing a contingency plan.

Designing a concert is partly about artistic truth, but it is just as much about protecting the show's financial lifeline. You have to know the union rules, the promoter's expectations, the contractual obligations, and the penalties for failing to meet them. You have to protect the artist from losing money, the crew from being pushed into unpaid minutes, and the promoter relationship that determines whether the tour thrives. Most of the audience will never see how much engineering goes into hitting the exact minute every night, and they shouldn't. But if you fail, they'll feel it immediately in the rushed endings, the sloppy transitions, the tired crew, the stressed performer, and the invisible money hemorrhaging behind the scenes.

A perfectly timed show is invisible. It begins exactly when it should and ends exactly when it must. And the audience walks out thinking they witnessed something effortless, unaware of the immense precision beneath the surface that allowed the world you built to exist at all.

Directing Tech Rehearsals and Cue Runs

If designing the show is about building an emotional arc that fits inside a real-world clock, then tech rehearsals and cue runs are where that arc either locks into place or falls apart entirely. Just as you timed the songs and the moments between them, you now have to time the machinery that carries those moments. In concerts, the transitions are where most directors lose control of the narrative. We have already talked about how transitions between songs can make or break the emotional flow of the night, but here the issue becomes even more specific: those transitions are no longer theoretical ideas scribbled in a notebook. They're now physical events involving lights, stagehands, automation, props, video, playback, and musicians moving through space. And unless you approach them with the same rigor you applied to the songs themselves, the audience will fall out of the world you built the moment the music stops.

In traditional concert practice, transitions are treated like logistical necessities. Stagehands sprint in, cables are dragged across the floor, the lighting director snaps the stage into a new look, and the crew retreats as fast as possible. It's the NASCAR pit crew mentality—get in, fix the thing, get out. The problem is that the audience can feel that energy. They feel the rush, the scramble, the sense that the performance has paused and the "real" world has poked through the seams. You can build the most emotionally coherent scene imaginable, but if the next transition feels like a factory reset, everything collapses. The illusion breaks. The show suddenly smells like work.

A transition cannot feel like maintenance. It must feel like part of the narrative.

That's why tech rehearsals and cue runs are as much about timing as the rest of the show. Before a single performer appears, you need days—plural—just to let the lighting director, the stage crew, the scenic team, the automation operators, and the video department rehearse the transitions on their own. This is where they learn the choreography that makes a reset look like a continuation rather than a disruption. They need to understand not only what they're doing, but how long it should take and what emotional temperature the moment requires. If a transition pulls us from grief to elation, the crew needs to know that. If it moves us from stillness to aggression, they need to know that too. Their work becomes part of the emotional palette.

These rehearsals are where you teach the crew that transitions have tempo. Some transitions should feel like breath—slow, careful, intuitive. Others should feel like a flare—quick, sharp, and decisive. Even the quickest transition has a rhythm. If it's too fast, the moment feels cheap. If it's too slow, the audience's attention drifts or worse, shatters. The point is not speed. The point is coherence.

Once the crew has internalized the transitions, you repeat the entire process with the performers present. Blocking the performers into these transitions is non-negotiable. They need to know where they move, what they touch, how they travel through the darkness, what sightlines are in play, whether a crew member crosses their path, and how that movement feels in the emotional arc of the show. You're not just teaching them "exit left." You're teaching them the emotional physics of the scene change. And just like the crew, they have to learn the timing—how long it takes to walk from the mic to the riser, how long a costume change eats, how many seconds of darkness they can stand in before the tension snaps, and when the lights will signal the next moment.

This is where many shows fall apart. Directors often let performers wing it. Crews do their transitions as fast as possible. Lighting directors set new looks in a vacuum. And then, on opening night, every transition feels like a reset button instead of a continuation. The audience's attention is dropped on the floor, over and over again. They fall out of the world not because the songs are weak, but because the connective tissue was never rehearsed as performance.

To prevent that, you also need to step back and look at each scene in relation to the one before it and the one after it. Each scene exists in a chain, and each link offers opportunities for you to insert the work of setting or striking the next moment without breaking the world. When you examine that chain deliberately, you start to see small pockets of time—20 seconds here, a moment of darkness there, a stillness behind a performer's back—where a set piece could quietly move or a prop could vanish. If you can incorporate a stagehand as a background character during one of those moments, even better. That stagehand becomes part of the mise-en-scène while performing what would otherwise be an intrusive piece of labor. It buys you extra time, protects the transition from feeling rushed, and enriches the narrative by embedding the mechanics of the show into the world of the show. Suddenly, the work that would have broken the illusion is now sustaining it.

And this is also the moment in the process when you first discover which crew members are genuinely aligned with the production and which are simply executing tasks. Tech rehearsals expose everything. If someone is resistant, or skeptical, or plainly uninterested in the artistic intention, you will feel it here. Ideally, you replace them. But on tour, in reality, you often can't. So when a crew member insists that something cannot be done, instead of shutting them down, you ask how they would do it differently while still maintaining the emotional temperature you're trying to create. That question reframes the conversation. It moves the crew member from obstruction into collaboration. It acknowledges their expertise while reasserting your vision. In many cases, the solution they propose is workable, or better, because they understand the physical limitations of the stage in a way you never will. In other cases, the conversation alone is enough to shift their attitude toward the show. Either way, tech is where you figure out who is actually inside the world with you—and how to bring the rest along.

When you direct tech rehearsals and cue runs with timing and narrative in mind, something else happens: the transitions become scenes of their own. They stop being the blank spaces between songs and become the breaths, the dissolves, the emotional apertures that carry the audience from one chapter of the night to the next. A well-directed transition is a scene change the audience never consciously notices—because they never re-enter reality long enough to question it.

The audience only stays inside the world if you never let them leave it. Tech rehearsals are where you build the machinery to make that possible. Cue runs are where you test the timing until the performance stops feeling like a sequence of tasks and starts feeling like a living piece of theater. And the show only becomes seamless when the transitions are treated as moments of artistry rather than obstacles to be cleared as quickly as possible.

Using Video to Coach Performance

Since the 1970s, artists have relied on video as a kind of mirror—one that reveals the truth a performer can never fully see from inside their own body. As soon as portable video gear became affordable, musicians and directors began recording rehearsals, studying playback, and adjusting stage direction with a level of scrutiny that would have been unthinkable in the decades before. You can go on YouTube today and find rehearsal footage that was once deeply private: the Ramones running their set at blistering speed in a bare studio, Michael Jackson drilling choreography until the air seems to vibrate around him, Prince refining a single gesture over and over until it lands with absolute precision. Those videos weren't meant for fans—they were tools. They were the laboratory where artists refined timing, posture, intention, and the physical grammar of performance long before an audience arrived.

Legitimate theater has its own paradox in this zone. Actors are taught to play to the last row of the balcony, to throw their performance to the farthest corner of the house, and yet the eighth row center always remains the best seat. It is the only place where you see the truth of the actor's face while still feeling the composition of the stage. Too close and you lose the picture. Too far and you lose the detail. Theater tries to solve this contradiction with training and blocking, but it rarely solves it with documentation. Video, when used at all, is usually placed at a single point, and that point almost always approximates the "best seat in the house." What it does not approximate is the rest of the building—the places where most people actually sit.

What I want you to do is something different. You now have access to cheap, portable video gear: phones, tablets, tiny action cameras, lightweight mounts. Hang them from pipes overhead. Stick them in the corner of the balcony. Place them in your rehearsal space at the approximate heights and angles of box seats, dress circles, and even partially obstructed-view locations—the sightlines your audience would occupy in an actual theater. Frame the show from angles that exist in the real world: the seat behind a lighting truss, the one with a speaker stack in the way, the far left aisle where the performer is always at a diagonal. These angles used to be invisible to directors because the cost of capturing them was prohibitive. A single prosumer camera on a tripod was once a major line item in the budget. You took what you could get. Now you can get the whole room.

When you review these recordings, you begin to see the show from perspectives previous generations couldn't access. You'll see that a gesture that looks elegant from the center section looks muddled from the balcony. A moment of intimacy that works beautifully from the floor disappears entirely when seen from the wings. A lighting cue that feels warm and theatrical from one angle becomes a blinding wash from another. This is the gift of modern video: a map of viewports that reflects the actual way the audience experiences the show rather than the idealized version directors often imagine.

With all of these angles recorded, you can play back the run and look for problem areas exactly the way athletes review game footage. But this part is crucial: playback is for diagnosis, not public critique. You never give a performer notes in front of other people. Public notes feel like public judgment, and judgment kills trust. When you spot something that needs work, the first step is private reflection. Come up with a couple of possible solutions. Look at the moment from more than one angle. Make sure you genuinely understand what is wrong and why the performer might have done it that way in the first place. Only then do you pull a still frame from the recording, print it out, and write a short, specific note. Something like, "This move doesn't work from this angle—could we try it another way on the next run and see if it looks better?" The phrasing matters. It's collaborative, not accusatory. It invites investigation rather than assigning blame.

The point of using video this way is not to create surveillance; it's to create clarity. It gives performers access to information they cannot obtain from the stage. They can see the gaps, the moments that flatten, the gestures that vanish. They can also see what is working—the crispness of a silhouette, the power of a still pose, the elegance of a turn. And they can adjust with precision because they are now part of the same visual vocabulary you've been shaping.

The more angles you collect, the more complete your understanding becomes. And the more complete your understanding, the more confidently you and your performers can refine the show. You're all looking at the same image, solving the same puzzle, tracking the same emotional truth. Video becomes a tool not for correction but for shared authorship. It helps everyone see the production the way the audience will see it: from everywhere, not just the perfect seat in the center.

Chapter 15
Tech Days and Opening Night

Managing Load-In and Run-Throughs

In the previous chapter we talked about the concept of technical rehearsals—why they exist, what they solve, and how video becomes the only honest mirror you'll get in this process. Now we need to talk about what actually happens when the theory hits the floor. Load-in. First passes. First mistakes. The first time the show stops being imaginary and becomes a physical problem you have to solve with real bodies and real fatigue.

This is where everything starts to wobble if you don't control the room.

Start with the schedule. Two sessions a day. Not because it's elegant, but because it's the only structure that prevents people from falling apart before the show even exists. You get one focused session, then you stop. You eat. You reset. Then you get another session. Anything beyond that is fantasy. Long days at this stage don't build shows—they build resentment, sloppiness, and injuries.

Musicians, in particular, are vulnerable here. Most of them do not enjoy rehearsal. It's not personal. It's chemical. Their entire performance mechanism is built around adrenaline. A crowd cheers, they ignite. A warehouse with work lights and no applause does not ignite anything. If you don't address this directly, they'll assume something is wrong—either with themselves or with the process.

Actors have the opposite metabolism. They love rehearsal because rehearsal is the work. They get to try, fail, adjust, try again. Musicians

DOI: 10.4324/9781003679332-15

hear "again" and think "I'm doing something wrong." Actors hear "again" and think "I get to refine this."

You need to explain this difference on day one. Not delicately. Clearly. "This is not a performance. You are not supposed to feel electric. You are supposed to feel like you are learning the map." If you don't reframe the room, the musicians will chase adrenaline that is not available.

Another practical rule: start rehearsals in daylight. Not because daylight is magical, but because the "real world" runs on business hours. You will need vendors, deliveries, repairs, replacements, consultations, and emergency miracles. All of those people close at 5pm. If you begin rehearsing at 7pm., you are locking yourself in a box with no external support. Once the major problems are solved, you can shift into night rehearsals to match touring hours. But the early phase must happen when help exists.

And build the room properly. Put chairs around the perimeter. Not as an afterthought—deliberately. When people are not onstage, they should be watching. They should understand the full shape of the show they are helping build. Phones destroy that understanding instantly. If someone's attention is in their lap, they are not part of the world; they are a spectator in the wrong dimension.

Ask—politely, but non-negotiably—that phones stay away during runs. It's not punishment. It's coherence. A rehearsal room with attention in the air feels alive. A rehearsal room with attention on screens feels like everyone is waiting to go home.

Load-in and run-throughs are not about perfection. They are about alignment. You are teaching everyone what kind of world they're stepping into, what kind of process they're part of, and what kind of focus the show requires. Once the room understands that, the show can actually begin.

When the room is functioning, you can start running the show. This begins long before anyone sings a note. Make a list of every version of the show you need to rehearse—festival set, headline set, radio-friendly promo set, stripped-down acoustic set, whatever the tour requires. You should already have a setlist for each version. Then extract the core songs that appear in all versions and put them in one list; everything else goes in a second list. These lists are your spine. Without them, rehearsal becomes guesswork and panic.

The first day the artist arrives, keep it simple: run the core songs once, then run the additional songs once. That's it. You are not shaping the show yet—you are exposing all the basic technical problems so the crew can start fixing them. The next day, no music at all. Just blocking and transitions. If you need a third day for that, take it; transitions are where most concerts fall apart. Then you begin the cycle: a full run of version one (music, blocking, transitions), followed by runs of the alternate versions in the days that follow. Throughout all of this, everyone writes down every issue—artist, crew, band, you. No speeches, no interruptions. Just notes. The pile is more important than the opinions.

When you've accumulated enough data, you sit in a circle—literally—and go through the notes one by one. It will feel like group therapy because it is. You do this for a day or two, then you start fixing the notes scene by scene, another day or two. Then you run version one again. Then the alternates. New notes. Another circle. More fixes. You repeat this cycle until you run out of time or the show stabilizes—whichever comes first. Only then do you bring in outside eyes for a dress rehearsal. At that point, the show should be coherent enough that an outsider can actually see it, not just guess what it's supposed to be. You should listen patiently to the feedback given to you by the dress rehearsal audience but don't take it too seriously. There may be one or two useful pieces of information there, but most of it will be biased in some way that isn't representative of the general public. Thank everyone for their feedback and tell them you will relay it to the "team" to consider, which you will then intentionally proceed to forget to do.

Preparing for Chaos: What Can Go Wrong, and How to Fix It

If the previous section was about managing structure, this one is about managing everything that tries to destroy it. Because at this stage, chaos isn't an accident. It's a habit. Some people bring it with them the way other people bring water bottles or headphones. And the moment you start technical rehearsals, those people reveal themselves.

You already know the type.

They thrive on touring because touring rewards adrenaline, improvisation, and the constant surge of solving problems at the last possible second. They need chaos the way other people need coffee. In fact, chaos is their coffee. The more predictable the day is, the more uncomfortable they become. A quiet day feels like failure. A smooth load-in feels like boredom. They will generate difficulty simply to feel useful.

This is not malicious. It's neurological.

Touring rewires people. The cycle of crisis → fix → praise becomes a drug. Techs, performers, managers—anyone can get hooked. And once they're hooked, order feels wrong to them. Predictable systems feel suspicious. Plans feel like traps.

The result: they create problems where none exist.

A cable that has worked for three days "suddenly" becomes unreliable.

A cue that was fine yesterday is "mysteriously not responding."

A performer who has sung the same line for ten years "can't hear anything anymore."

None of this is sabotage. It's autopilot chaos. And unless you address it, the chaos becomes the weather system of the room.

Your job is not to eliminate chaos—it never goes away. Your job is to prevent it from steering the process.

Start by identifying the source. Chaos addicts always share the same tells:

They speak in emergencies.
They bring you problems without bringing you solutions.
They escalate before they investigate.
They interrupt rehearsal flow to announce issues that could easily wait.
They present minor glitches as existential threats.

Once you spot them, you do not reprimand them. You redirect them.

Say, "Great. Log it. We'll solve it in the break."

This single sentence destroys their power. Chaos cannot survive when it is scheduled. You fold their emergency into the structure and the emergency stops being interesting to them.

Another tactic: assign ownership.

Chaos thrives in ambiguity. If no one is responsible for a task, everyone becomes reactive. Give the chaos addict something measurable and boring—inventory, cross-checking cues, documenting settings. Chaos addicts hate documentation because documentation eliminates heroism. And without heroism, their favorite identity dissolves.

Most of what "goes wrong" in tech isn't actual failure—it's unmanaged expectation. Equipment will malfunction. Batteries will die. Wireless will drop. Screens will flicker. Instruments will need adjustment. These things are part of the medium, not signs of doom. What destroys rehearsals isn't the problem—it's the drama around the problem.

A director who panics gives permission for everyone else to panic. A director who treats the problem as inevitable gives permission for everyone else to stay focused. When something breaks, your first job is to keep the room calm. Not by pretending the issue doesn't matter, but by framing it correctly:

"This is normal. We expected this. Keep going until I say stop."

Chaos addicts depend on the assumption that every glitch requires an immediate halt. Break that assumption. If a light is wrong but not dangerous, keep going. If a monitor mix is off but the performer can still sing safely, keep going. If the projector freezes during a run-through, finish the run and fix it after. Stopping is the most expensive action in rehearsal. You must protect the run-through at all costs.

Because here is the truth: most chaos in tech is not technical. It's emotional. It's people managing their anxiety by pushing it onto the process. Your job is to absorb the anxiety without letting it shape the day.

A rehearsal room that survives chaos is not a calm room—it's a room where the chaos has nowhere to attach itself.

Final Polish and Preshow Briefings

If you have the luxury of taking a couple of days off before the final run-through, take it. At this stage you are so deep inside the show you can't see straight. You've spent days watching the same transitions, the same cues, the same problems cycling through different disguises. Your brain has stopped evaluating and has started hallucinating. A short break is the only way to reset your eyes. Without that distance, your final run-through is just another rehearsal and you will walk into opening night with no actual sense of what you've made.

If you don't have the luxury—and most people don't—then end the last rehearsal day early. Not politely early. Meaningfully early. Give people enough time to go home, shower, eat real food, stare at a wall, or simply exist as civilians for a few hours. You need oxygen in the system before opening night. A show that is pressed straight from rehearsal into performance without any breath becomes brittle. It plays tight. It fights itself. A little space lets the show settle into its actual form.

Any persistent issues—the ones that have survived every note session and still feel like small fires—bring them up in a preshow meeting. Not to solve them. To acknowledge them. Once everyone knows the weak spots, the entire company can support them instead of being blindsided. Sometimes awareness is the fix. Sometimes the fix is simply that everyone is paying attention to the same crack in the pavement.

And then there are the outside interests. The label. The promoter. The management rep who suddenly "remembers" a conversation from six months ago and insists that a particular song "has to be in the show." Smile. Agree. Nod. Then do whatever you were going to do anyway. Touring has one great advantage over every other branch of performance: the cycle moves too fast for anyone to track their own demands. After 48 hours, no one remembers what they insisted on. By the time you hit the second city, the complaint has evaporated, the setlist has stabilized, and the only thing that matters is whether the audience was moved in some way by the performance.

Final polish isn't about perfection. It's about clearing the static so the show can breathe. You've built the machine. Now you just need to get out of its way.

Chapter 16
Touring with a Directed Show

Maintaining Consistency Across Dates

Once the show is built, your next job is making sure it stays built. This sounds obvious, but it's the part most directors neglect because they assume they'll be there every night to steer things back on course. You won't. At some point you will be in another city, on another project, or simply unavailable, and the show will have to run without you. Someone else—an associate, a stage manager, a well-meaning tech, or an eager new hire—will suddenly become "the person in charge," whether they're prepared or not.

If you haven't documented the show clearly, the show will begin to drift. Not intentionally. Drift is subtle. A gesture gets a little bigger. A cue creeps a few beats later. Someone tries something "just to see if it works." The crew responds to the performers instead of the plan. After three or four dates, the show you built has been replaced by a souvenir version of itself—familiar, but slightly warped.

Your only defense against drift is documentation. Boring, unglamorous, indispensable documentation. Every choice you've made must now exist somewhere outside your brain. Not as poetry, not as theory—as instructions. You're building a manual that allows someone else to preserve your reasoning even when they can't ask you questions. The lighting design (and its intent), the staging, the alternates you rehearsed, the rules about where improvisation is allowed and where it absolutely isn't. Write it all down. If you stepped off the tour tomorrow, someone

DOI: 10.4324/9781003679332-16

should be able to pick up your packet and know exactly what happens and why.

This documentation should be kept (and backed up) in three ways. First, use visual collaboration software (e.g., Milanote, Miro, Notion, or Trello). This provides the greatest flexibility for detailing all original ideas. Second, create a PDF handbook with an index. Third, print hard copies of both for emergencies.

With advancing AI technology, it may also be beneficial to input everything into an AI agent so that a substitute director could query it to resolve an urgent problem.

Once the tour actually starts, the rhythm of the road gives you a different kind of time—more scattered, but strangely abundant. You can usually look three or four shows ahead and start scouting venues long before you arrive. This is when consistency becomes a proactive job. Every venue has its own personality, and some have personality disorders. To avoid surprises, you start building a habit of venue research: "A View from My Seat" for sightlines, recent YouTube clips of comparable tours, audience photos, local reviews, Ticketmaster comments—anything that gives you a sense of what will interfere with the show you've designed.

You're not researching for curiosity; you're researching to spot the traps before they spring. Low ceilings, obstructed balconies, shallow stages, strange overhangs, dead zones in the PA, house screens you can't turn off. Once you know what's coming, you look at the alternate versions of scenes you have already rehearsed and choose which ones this venue requires. When you arrive on show day, you're not discovering problems—you're notifying everyone of the solutions that were already planned.

Meanwhile, the performers need to know you're still watching. Even if everything went beautifully the night before, you still give notes. The note can be a single sentence. It can even be, "Great work tonight." The content matters less than the signal. Performers notice when no one is paying attention, and the moment they believe no one is paying attention, they start testing the boundaries. Not maliciously—human nature. Daily notes keep them inside the world you built instead of building a new one of their own.

Consistency isn't about policing. It's about attention. When everyone knows the show is still being directed, the show remains directed.

Teaching the Crew to Preserve Your Direction

The only thing worse than a show drifting is a show drifting because the people who were supposed to guard it didn't know what they were guarding. The crew can't preserve your direction if they don't know what your direction is in practical terms, not poetic ones.

Start with the tour manager. They are the person who actually runs the tour, which means they are the person who decides who steps into your role when you're somewhere else. Don't leave this ambiguous. Ask directly: Who takes over when I'm not here? A tech? A stage manager? A production assistant? The person who happens to be closest to the comms system? Whoever it is, you and the tour manager need to agree on this before the first show loads in. If you don't, the job will default to whoever volunteers, and that person will inevitably give notes based on what they prefer, not what you directed.

Once you know who your substitute is, sit down with them and the tour manager together. This is not a private conversation; it's a structural one. You're not just training a person—you're creating a chain of custody for the show. The goal is simple: teach them how to think like you think, at least in the narrow slice of reality that applies to the show.

You show them how to read your documentation, how to interpret your notes, what the "non-negotiables" look like, and how to tell the difference between a performer making a choice and a performer forgetting a cue. You're not teaching them to direct—you're teaching them to recognize deviations. If something shifts, they need to know whether it's a mistake, an improvisation, or a problem.

Then you talk about video. Video is the only way you can monitor the show when you aren't physically there, so you have to be specific about what you want. Do you want a wide shot from front-of-house? A lateral angle so you can see spacing? A tight shot of a particular choreography moment? A recording of the LED wall for sync issues? Don't make them guess. Tell them exactly what you need so you don't spend your night watching shaky footage of someone's head blocking the downstage left riser.

And then, most importantly, you tell them how you want to receive notes when you return to the tour. This is the part directors forget. If you come back and everyone floods you with three weeks' worth of scattered observations, you'll spend days unraveling chaos instead of stepping into a clear picture. So decide now:

Do you want a nightly summary?
A bullet list of only the major changes?
Notes organized by department?
A top-three "things that drifted" list?
A video link and a timestamped breakdown?

You're teaching them to filter information the way you do so you don't walk back into a cloud of subjective opinions disguised as "help."

The crew doesn't need to be miniature versions of you. They just need to understand the map well enough to keep the show from wandering off the road. If they can do that, your direction survives even when you aren't there to enforce it—and that is the real measure of whether a show has been directed well.

Adapting on the Fly

Even with all your preparation, all your documentation, and all your neatly filed contingency plans, something is still going to go wrong. Not "might." Will. Touring looks predictable from the outside, but every date contains variables you can't fully control, no matter how prepared you are. Your job isn't to prevent problems (that's actually the tour manager's job); your job is to keep the show's world intact when the problems arise.

The first step is admitting that problems will happen in categories. A lighting problem is different from a sound problem. A performer problem is different from a venue problem. Weather is its own unpredictable category. Each one breaks the show in a different way and requires a different kind of triage. Before the tour even leaves the rehearsal studio, you should know which problems can be fixed quietly backstage, which ones require a major adjustment, and which ones have the potential to delay or cancel a show entirely.

Delay or cancellation is its own event. When that happens, there will be someone—again, the tour manager—telling the social media person what to post. But the show does not end at the curtain line. The world you've created extends outward: merch, marketing, the pre-show audio, the visuals, and yes, the voice of every public-facing message. If the show is built on vulnerability and intimacy, a generic "Due to unforeseen circumstances ..." post fractures that world. So you need that language written in advance. Not flowery, not dramatic—just aligned. Aligned with the tone of the show and with the character of the artist. If an announcement has to go out in a crisis, it should still sound like it belongs to the same universe the audience paid to enter. That message may be a part of the show if it is to be rescheduled.

And then there are the problems that happen onstage. A broken light can be ignored. A broken LED panel can be worked around. But what happens if the drummer breaks an arm? What if the guitarist gets sick? What if the lead loses their voice mid-tour? These aren't theoretical questions; they happen more often than anyone wants to admit. When the drum tech steps in, they will know how to play the parts—but they won't know the story. They won't know the blocking that isn't musical, the cues that signal transitions, the moments where the drummer is part of the scene rather than part of the band. If you don't prepare a cheat sheet for this—written, clear, and rehearsed when everyone is calm—you will be trying to teach someone the second layer of their job while the first layer is already on fire.

Decide now: if someone needs to be replaced mid-tour, what time of day do you run a crash rehearsal? Where do you hold it? Who runs it? Which cues are essential and which ones can be simplified? You don't want to make these decisions at 3pm. in a dark arena while catering rolls in lunch and everyone is panicking.

This is why you sit down with the tour manager before any of this happens. The tour manager will have their own set of contingency plans—operational, logistical, safety-related. Your job is to translate those plans into the world of the show. A generator failure doesn't just mean "We can't power the rig." It means, "How do we keep the emotional shape of the night intact if we have to strip the show down to its bones?" A venue evacuation doesn't just mean "The show will resume when law enforcement clears it." It means, "What is the first image the audience sees when they come back, and does it match the world?"

Use every tool available—common sense, previous tour disasters, local quirks, your darkest imagination—and make a list of the worst things that could realistically happen. Not to indulge anxiety, but to eliminate improvisation under pressure. Discuss that list with the tour manager and build thematic adaptations that feel like they belong inside the show's reality. If you have to scale something down, it should feel intentional. If you have to cut something, it should feel like a choice. Even in crisis, the world holds.

Adapting on the fly is not about heroics. It's about refusing to break the spell, no matter what breaks around you.

Chapter 17
Concerts as Art, Though Commerce Pays

Reclaiming Creative Space in a Monetized World

For the last 20 years, the concert industry has been drifting in one direction: toward the spreadsheet. Not because anyone set out to make concerts less artistic, but because corporate oversight—promoters, ticketing companies, conglomerate venue chains, touring insurers, VIP package providers—has steadily wrapped itself around every corner of the live-music ecosystem. With that oversight came money. Real money. Bigger budgets, bigger rooms, bigger lights, bigger everything. And for a while it felt like a blessing: "Look how much more we can build now."

But there's a cost to money that no one likes to talk about. Money takes space. It expands into every crack of the working day until it pushes art into the margins. And that's what has happened to concerts. Production values have ballooned, but artistic expression—actual expression, the part that comes from the world you're building, not the rig you're flying—has barely grown at all. In some cases it has shrunk.

There was a time when bands like R.E.M. and Pearl Jam could walk into an arena and say, "Black out the building. No ads. No banners. No corporate noise." And the venue would do it. Not because they were generous, but because the artist's cultural gravity outranked the arena's sponsorship obligations. Today that's virtually impossible. The walls now belong to someone else: beverage sponsors, credit-card partners, mobile carriers, sportsbook apps, insurance brands. Even the

DOI: 10.4324/9781003679332-17

railings and stairs have logos. The building is a billboard, and the show has to squeeze itself in between the ads.

This is the environment you inherit as a director. You are building a world inside a world that is already for sale.

So your job is not to wage war against commerce—you won't win that war, and you don't need to. Your job is to reclaim creative space inside a monetized landscape without threatening the income streams that keep the tour afloat. The goal is not purity. The goal is integrity. You build the show's world so vividly, so intentionally, that commerce becomes a compliant guest rather than an intrusive landlord.

And that reclamation begins long before doors open.

Most venues now charge an "early entry" or "express entry" fee, which is fine in theory—people pay for convenience, and convenience has value. But the way it's usually executed is a mess. Audiences stand outside in hot, disorganized lines, clumped against barricades, waiting for a set of doors that will not open for 40 minutes. Nothing about that experience connects to the world you have built inside. The first moments of the night—the moments when the audience should be entering the story—are instead an obstacle course of wristbands, metal detectors, and vague instructions shouted by exhausted security staff.

The industry calls this "VIP." It isn't.

VIP packages often include merchandise that has nothing to do with the performance, meet-and-greets that satisfy neither the artist nor the fan, and photo ops that feel like airport security with better lighting. These things exist because they make money, not because they make sense. And if you don't address them early in the process of writing the show, they will erode the world before the audience even crosses the threshold.

Fixing this doesn't require a revolution; it requires intentionality.

Imagine a line where cast members—real cast members from the world of the show—work alongside venue staff. Not in costume necessarily, but in tone. Using the show's vocabulary. Welcoming audience members with the same emotional temperature that exists onstage. Think of it like hosting a dinner party: no one should arrive standing alone, staring at their shoes. A good host circulates. A good host connects strangers. A good host sets the tone before the meal begins.

A cast member says one line to the people waiting outside and the world starts before they've walked through the metal detector.

When done correctly, it's the circus-comes-to-town effect: the feeling that something has arrived—something vibrant, something alive—and that anyone who gets a taste of it will want to run away and join it the next morning.

This same principle applies to transparency around set times.

Venues often post the door time as the event time because it forces people to arrive early and spend money—on drinks, on snacks, on merch, on anything that keeps the per-caps healthy. And yes, per-caps matter. They fund your show indirectly. They keep venues happy. They help tours survive.

But there's a difference between encouraging spending and exhausting the audience.

If someone spends two hours standing in a crowded lobby waiting for a show to start, they're not entering your world—they're draining their energy so they can survive theirs. People have jobs the next morning. They have babysitters waiting at home. They have real-life responsibilities they can't ignore just because someone decided that "doors at 7" should secretly mean "show at 9:20."

Everything we can do to reduce that friction buys us receptivity. And receptivity buys us the show.

A receptive audience is more open, more moved, more willing to go where you lead them. And ironically—this is the part venues often forget—a receptive audience spends more money. Not because they were tricked, but because they feel good. Because they are having a good night. Because the world you built has taken care of them instead of draining them.

So you find a way—early, clearly, intentionally—to communicate set times in a way that is mutually beneficial to both venue and artist. You make the case that clarity is not the enemy of revenue; exhaustion is. When the show respects the audience's time, the audience rewards everyone.

This is what reclaiming creative space looks like. Not purity. Not rebellion. Not refusing to engage with commerce. Instead, it's about protecting the emotional architecture of the night—from the first wristband to the last note—so the world of the show can actually breathe inside the world that pays for it.

Artistry vs. Sales vs. Sponsorship

The modern touring economy depends on sales. It depends on sponsorship. It depends on revenue streams that did not even exist 20 years ago—VIP upsells, premium seating tiers, brand activations, experiential marketing zones, drink partnerships, credit-card presales, and whatever new acronym someone invents next quarter. These things aren't optional add-ons. They are structural. They are the reason most shows can afford to exist at the scale they do.

So the point is not to pretend you can build a hermetically sealed, commerce-free utopia. You can't. And if you try, you will collapse under your own purity. The money is real. The money is necessary. The trick is understanding that commerce cannot be allowed to drive the show's behavior, only support it.

And this is where many productions lose the plot—literally.

Left unchecked, sponsorship will insinuate itself into the emotional architecture of the night. Not because sponsors are malicious, but because sponsorship is a business of visibility. They are used to placing logos on anything that holds still long enough. They buy presence, not context. They assume that if something exists in the building, they can put their name on it.

Your job is to stop them—politely, firmly, consistently—because there is one boundary that must never be crossed:

Sponsorship cannot enter the show itself.

Not the story, not the staging, not the set, not the illusions, not the world.

Once a brand steps into the inner world of the show, the world collapses.

There is no faster way to turn a transcendental moment into a supermarket aisle.

The audience won't blame the sponsor's marketing rep.

They will blame the show.

They will blame the artist.

They will blame you.

So you draw the line. Calmly. Without panic. You explain that the world of the show is a fragile ecosystem, and anything that breaks its internal logic—any logo, any tagline, any "brought to you by"—will be felt to be an intrusion. And that intrusion reflects poorly on the brand, not well. The sponsor doesn't want to be the villain who ruined the night. You're not fighting them; you're protecting them from themselves.

Most of the time, that is enough.

If a sponsor absolutely insists on some presence near the show's content—and occasionally they do—you do not give them a blank stage. You find a creative container that absorbs the intrusion. You build a frame. You design a context. You make sure the audience experiences the moment as a stylistic choice, not a commercial interruption. And even then, you push to keep the sponsor's presence out of anything that resembles story.

Because once the world is broken, it's broken. You cannot unbreak it.

Artistry, sales, and sponsorship are not three opposing forces. They are three bodies orbiting the same night. The mistake is assuming that they need equal weight. They don't. Artistry is the gravity. Sales and sponsorship are satellites. When artistry leads, everything else aligns around it naturally. When sales lead, the show becomes a commercial installation with a band attached. When sponsorship leads, the show becomes a themed corporate conference with pyrotechnics.

Your job is to restore the correct hierarchy.

The show comes first.

The world comes first.

Meaning comes first.

The money can stay—there's room for it—but it stays in the real world, not the imagined one. And when sponsors understand that protecting the world actually increases the audience's goodwill, and goodwill increases the audience's openness, and openness increases the audience's spending, the argument stops being philosophical and becomes obvious.

Artistry isn't the enemy of commerce. It's the thing that makes the commerce work.

Elevating the Medium

Earlier in this book, I made a blunt claim: the medium of live music has been stagnant for 30 years. In some corners it has even regressed. That wasn't exaggeration. If you step back far enough and strip away the noise—ticketing systems, LED walls, marketing campaigns, social media cycles—you will see that the fundamental shape of most large-scale concerts has barely evolved since the late 1990s. In many cases, it has simplified. The gear got bigger. The budgets got bigger. But the ideas stayed the same.

Most major pop tours today are essentially runway shows with a soundtrack. Costume changes, thematic "eras," maximalist screens, glossy moving set pieces, and a performer standing at the front of a gigantic corporate installation. The audience is not entering a story; they are watching a sequence of highly branded tableaus. It is visual fashion with music attached. And because the same vendors supply the same technology to everyone, the shows start to blend together. You can walk into any arena in any American city and see the exact same automation tricks, the same LED vocabulary, the same lighting palettes, the same choreography beats. The artists are different. The shows are not.

This is not the crew's fault. This is not even the artists' fault. This is what happens when an industry follows the path of least resistance for long enough. It becomes self-referential. It starts designing by precedent. "What did the last big tour do?" becomes the design brief. Risk disappears. The medium stops evolving because the machine that produces it is too large, too expensive, and too intertwined with corporate interests to make genuine creative leaps on its own.

This is where the director comes in.

Your job—maybe your most important job—is to elevate the medium. Not to decorate it. Not to imitate it. To push it. Drag it forward. Tear it open. To create something the audience didn't know they wanted because they've never seen it before.

If you are only looking at what is on the road right now, you are already behind. You're designing inside a shrinking circle. You're participating in a loop of recycled aesthetics that had their meaning stripped away three tours ago. The point is not to "fit in." The point is not to prove you understand the current touring vocabulary. The point is to expand the vocabulary.

Everyone else is standing on the outside looking in.

Your job is to stand on the outside looking farther out.

When you do this correctly, you stop competing with the trends. You stop competing with other tours. You stop competing with the marketplace of spectacle. You're not trying to outperform the LED wall arms race; you're opting out of it entirely and building a visual language that belongs only to this artist, this story, this world.

Elevating the medium does not mean spending more money. It means spending your attention differently. It means asking questions other people have stopped asking:

Why is this the default shape of a concert?
What if the most powerful moment of the show has no lights at all?
What happens if we bring the audience into the story physically rather than just visually?
What if the most "expensive" idea is actually the smallest one done perfectly?
What can we say that no one else on the road has the courage to say?

These questions sound abstract, but their answers are intensely practical. They determine how you build the room, how you stage transitions, how you use silence, how you pace the show, how you frame the performer, how you deploy color, how you treat the audience. They become the design principles that make your show impossible to confuse with anyone else's.

There are two paths you can take as a concert director:

1 Follow the industry's habits and become another voice echoing its limitations.
2 Redefine the perimeter of what the medium can do and make the industry catch up.

The first is easier. The second is the job.

I'm not asking you to reinvent the history of live music every night. But I am asking you to look at the medium as something elastic, not fixed. Something unfinished, not standardized. Something that needs your imagination more than your compliance.

Audiences can tell when a show is designed from obligation. They can smell safety. They can feel when the production was built around not offending anyone—artist, manager, promoter, crew chief, brand partner. And they are polite about it. They applaud. They take their photos. They tell their friends it was "amazing." But they forget it almost instantly.

What they remember—what changes the medium—is the night when something unexpected happened. When the show didn't feel like a product line. When the world they stepped into felt alive, intentional, and specific. When they felt the presence of an idea.

Your job is to create that presence.

Not because it's rebellious.

Not because it's fashionable.

Because if we don't elevate the medium, the medium will evaporate into commerce.

And then there will be nothing left to direct.

Chapter 18
Why So Few Concerts Have Directors (and How to Change That)

A Historical Look at How Concerts Evolved without Directors

If you want to understand why so few concerts today have directors, you have to start by looking backward—not at the recent stadium spectacles or the blockbuster tours, but at the earliest versions of the live pop show. And the simplest truth is this: concerts did not evolve with directors because, for a long time, they didn't need them.

In the early days of pop music, a live performance rarely lasted long enough to require an architect. The industry was singles-driven; artists toured as part of larger revues, sharing the bill with half a dozen other acts, each one delivering a tightly compressed, three-song sprint. The show was essentially a musical variety hour performed in fragments. There was no "evening" to shape, no arc to build, no emotional terrain to cross. The songs were the unit, not the concert.

Those three songs, however, were meticulously choreographed—out of necessity rather than artistry. The choreography had to function on two simultaneous fronts: television and technology. Performers had to stay in the frame of early TV cameras, which meant staging from the waist up. And they had to remain glued to microphones that could not track movement, which meant almost no travel onstage. What looked like simplicity was actually constraint. Performers had to look alive while barely moving.

So the only "director" in this era was the person responsible for staging one or two songs for broadcast. A de facto director, not a theatrical one. Someone hired to design gestures that read well on eight-inch

DOI: 10.4324/9781003679332-18

screens. Lana Del Rey's languid, front-facing TV posture—often mistaken for affect—is actually a modern repurposing of this exact technique: perform for the camera, not the room.

Early rock and roll cracked open this model, but only slightly. The Beatles still inherited the vocabulary of the revue. Their infamous "Beatle Bow," that synchronized forward bend at the end of a performance, is not a rock gesture at all—it's a vaudeville artifact. An afterimage of a world where the performance was a routine, not a journey.

As concerts stretched longer, the lack of direction became more conspicuous. The Grateful Dead were the purest form of this evolutionary branch: a band that rejected the very idea of planning. Their shows reached three hours not because of theatrical ambition but because improvisation demanded stamina. Without a director, they instinctively invented their own version of structure. An intermission. Later, a dedicated drum segment that acted as a second intermission—a functional pause disguised as an artistic choice, giving the rest of the band time to drink water, go to the bathroom, stay upright. There were lighting operators, yes, but no cues in the theatrical sense. No sequence. No dramaturgy. The show happened, and the operators reacted.

Yet the Dead and their contemporaries pushed the technology of live sound and lighting so far that a new possibility emerged: concerts could now hold shape. And once that possibility existed, someone had to give it form.

Pink Floyd was among the first to treat concerts not as gigs but as staged experiences. For the first time, lighting cues had to hit specific moments. Films had to sync. Inflatable set pieces had to arrive on musical downbeats rather than at the whim of a stagehand. This was not direction as theater yet, but it was the beginning of direction as necessity.

From there, the next generation—KISS, Parliament-Funkadelic, Alice Cooper—did what innovators always do: they borrowed expertise from other worlds. They hired designers from Broadway, from the circus, from spaces where a show was not merely performed but built. And those designers brought with them stagecraft, process, and, inevitably, directors. KISS was the first major rock act to tour with something that resembled a fully directed show. Alice Cooper went further, raiding the visual grammar of Disney and the physical language of vaudeville. Suddenly, a concert could behave like a play if you wanted it to.

Then MTV arrived and changed the expectation entirely. Audiences now met the artist first on camera—larger than life, tightly edited, visually sculpted. When they bought tickets, they expected the person they'd seen on TV. Not a human with a guitar. A persona. A world. And so the medium shifted. Sets got bigger. Costumes got louder. Hair metal, for all its excess, was essentially a Broadway musical disguised as heavy metal: narrative impressions, stylized silhouettes, and staging choices borrowed from theater and repainted with neon.

At the same time, the supernova tours of Madonna, Michael Jackson, and Prince set a template that 90 percent of modern pop tours still borrow from—choreographed spectacle tied to persona, reinforced by screens, driven by story logic whether the audience recognizes it or not. Queen blended rock with opera while repurposing staging techniques from magic shows; the Stones inherited and adapted opera staging into their own touring infrastructure, where it remained for nearly 20 years. These were not "directed" shows in the theatrical sense, but they were no longer random. Someone was making decisions about shape.

As the technology advanced further—and MTV's power to sell tours evaporated—concerts drifted into another phase. They became demonstrations of equipment. Moving lights, lasers, automated risers, deployable walls. Rigs grew smarter; planning became more technical. As a result, technical directors and lighting designers quietly assumed creative control. The show followed the rig, not the performer. Direction became something you did with consoles, not bodies.

Only in the last decade did the pendulum swing again. Touring budgets ballooned. Insurance liability skyrocketed. Artists became brands with fiscal obligations not to get injured or sick. And suddenly choreographers and musical directors became the de facto architects—not for narrative purposes, but to manage risk. The priority shifted to maximizing the feeling of proximity to the performer while minimizing the actual physical demands on them. A show became a distribution problem: how to ration the artist's time onstage without diminishing the illusion of their presence.

Every era has exceptions. Every rule has an outlier. But the broad sweep is clear: concerts evolved without directors because their earliest forms did not require direction. And by the time they did, other people—camera operators, lighting designers, choreographers, technicians—had already filled the vacuum.

Direction never entered the medium by design. It entered by accident.

Why Concerts Turned into Logistics Problems instead of Artistic Problems

If you want to understand why concerts stopped being artistically led, you have to understand the moment they became logistically led. It didn't happen abruptly. There was no day when managers gathered in a hotel ballroom and declared that art would henceforth take a back seat to truck space. It happened quietly, gradually, and almost invisibly—through the accumulation of practical decisions that, one by one, redefined the purpose of the entire enterprise.

The simple truth is that once concerts grew big enough to require fleets of trucks, union crews, automation systems, LED walls, rigging teams, pyro specialists, carpenters, electricians, and safety officers, the show stopped being built around what the artist wanted to express and started being built around what the production could physically execute in the available time.

Load-in times replaced emotional beats.

Truck packs replaced storyboards.

Safety briefings replaced dramaturgy.

The questions that once guided a show—What is the emotional arc? What is the world of the performance? What should the audience feel at this moment?—were quietly replaced by questions of a very different nature:

How long will the LED wall take to assemble?
Can the scenic elements be stored on the sides of the stage?
How many automation operators do we need if the riser moves more than 12 inches?
Will this effect violate local fire codes in Cleveland?

None of these questions are unreasonable. They are essential. But they are not artistic. And over time, the logistical questions became the only questions that were consistently asked, because they were the only ones that could be answered reliably. Logistics, unlike artistry, has codified rules: weights, limits, measurements, labor calls, power requirements, truck dimensions. Logistics tells you what is possible. Art asks what is meaningful.

But in the touring world "possible" won.

Part of the problem is structural. Touring schedules are built on speed: one show ends at 11pm, the trucks load until 3am, the crew drives through the night, and by 10am they are unloading into the next venue. There is no time for rehearsal. There is no time for revision. There is barely time to eat. So the show cannot evolve artistically once it leaves rehearsals—because the conditions of the tour make artistic thinking impractical. What can evolve, and what does evolve, are the logistical plans. And over time, they dominate the aesthetic simply because they are the only flexible system still in motion.

Another factor is power. The people who control logistics—production managers, crew chiefs, riggers, carpenters—control the feasibility of the show. Their decisions determine what can or cannot exist. Not because they are creatively hostile, but because they are tasked with preventing disaster. If a scenic element is too heavy, it is cut. If a lighting truss cannot fly safely, it is redesigned. If pyro creates a hazard, the pyro goes. These are sensible choices. But when every creative idea must first pass through a technical feasibility filter, eventually only ideas that suit the filter get proposed.

In that environment, art becomes the residue of what logistics permits.

This is how the modern concert became a creature of engineering: the emotional architecture of the night is determined by how long it takes to strike the drum riser, or how much weight the ceiling can carry, or whether the screens need a three-minute reset between content packages.

What the audience sees is the byproduct of what can be loaded, rigged, flown, and operated safely—and fast.

The result is that many shows feel similar not because artists lack imagination, but because the logistical systems governing them are nearly identical. The same venues. The same weight limits. The same trucking companies. The same lighting rigs. The same labor rules. The same touring templates. It is not that creativity has disappeared—it is that creativity has been forced to conform to the shape of the machinery.

And because logistics are quantifiable and art is not, the industry naturally drifted toward the thing it could measure, predict, and insure.

This is the quiet tragedy of modern touring: concerts became logistical achievements long before they became artistic ones.

The people running the shows were not artists; they were problem-solvers. Brilliant, skilled, indispensable problem-solvers—but not directors. And without someone advocating for the story, the story faded from view.

Advocacy for Formalized Direction in Musical Performance

If concerts are ever going to reclaim their artistic potential, someone has to hold the job that no one else on the tour is trained—or incentivized—to do: someone has to think about the show as a unified experience rather than a sequence of solvable problems. Someone has to be responsible for the concepts, the designs, the pacing, the emotional arc, the meaning behind the spectacle. And that someone is the director.

But a director in the concert world must work differently from a director in theater. You are not operating in a space built for artistry; you are operating in a space built for forklifts, timecode, union calls, and rigging points. Your ideas cannot live in the abstract. They must pass through the hands of carpenters, automation technicians, loaders, rigger crews, electricians, and video engineers. If they cannot survive that journey, then they are not ideas—they are burdens.

This is why the most effective concert directors do not think in terms of giant transformations or monumental stagecraft. They think in small, durable ideas—ideas simple enough that a construction worker could look at them and say, "Yeah, we can do that," but resonant enough that an audience would weep without understanding why.

A director's task is to find those ideas.

You build a show not by overpowering the logistical machine, but by slipping your vision into its empty spaces. By crafting moments that are emotionally huge but technically microscopic. A change of silhouette. A shift in color temperature. A performer crossing from shadow into light at a specific lyric. A screen not exploding with imagery, but going silent at the exact moment the audience expects noise. A prop as small as a glass of water, handled with ritual. A single word whispered instead of shouted.

These are the places where direction lives: not in the fireworks but in the negative space around them.

When you design the overall arc of a concert, you are not building a castle; you are building a spine. A simple, unbreakable structure that everything else—the lights, the sound, the choreography, the scenic elements, even the venues themselves—can wrap themselves around. You are crafting something so clear and so sturdy that no matter what happens on the road, no matter which truss goes down or which automation cue misfires, the show still has shape.

Because the truth is that a directed concert does not rely on any single effect. It relies on intention.

A director's job is to ask:

What is the emotional journey the audience must travel?
Where does the performer transform?
What is the one moment of grace the audience will carry home?

And then to build those moments with materials that are impossible to break: light, silence, stillness, breath.

The most powerful ideas in live performance are always the ones that feel inevitable. They feel as if no other choice could have been made. But that inevitability comes from the director doing the work long before the trucks ever leave the warehouse—thinking through how the idea touches everything that came before it, how it evolves it, how it fits the show's heartbeat and the backstage reality, how it avoids every possible logistical conflict while still delivering a blow straight to the audience's chest.

When a director does this well, the crew looks at the plan and sees simplicity. The audience looks at the performance and sees wonder. And the artist, standing in the middle of it all, feels held by something larger than themselves—a world built for them, around them, and with them.

That is the role concerts have been missing.

That is the discipline capable of stitching together chaos into meaning.

That is the future of musical performance, if the industry chooses it.

A show becomes art when someone takes responsibility for its soul.

And a director is simply the person brave enough to say:

"I will keep the soul intact."

Chapter 19
When the Artist Doesn't Want Direction

How to Collaborate with Artists Who "Don't Need Help"

In this section I'd like to talk about what to do if you find yourself directing a show against the artist's will. This may occur if an investor, label executive, or promoter hires you to work on the show. This might also occur if everyone on the tour is onboard (as we discussed earlier in the book) but then later on one of the cast members (a drummer, bassist, or percussionist, for example) starts to ignore their commitment to the work.

The first and most important thing to understand about an artist who insists they "don't need direction" is that they are not posturing. They are not challenging your authority. They are not rejecting the idea of collaboration. They are simply articulating the only reality the industry has ever allowed them to know. Popular music produces a particular kind of success story—one where talent is validated long before craft is learned, where instinct substitutes for method, and where the absence of formal training is not a disadvantage but a prerequisite. Unlike theater, where actors train for years, or film, where directors apprentice under other directors, pop artists often rise to visibility with no artistic foundation beyond whatever impulses got them noticed in the first place. The system discovers them early, accelerates them violently, and then treats every idiosyncrasy as evidence of genius.

This trajectory creates a psychological architecture that is not pathological but is absolutely distorted. You cannot be adored by millions

DOI: 10.4324/9781003679332-19

and accommodated by everyone in your orbit without experiencing some degree of emotional contortion. Sustained fame bends a person's perception of risk, of self, of reality. It isolates them, cocoons them, and turns even ordinary decisions into high-stakes performances. The pressure reshapes their nervous system. The reward structure warps their sense of accuracy. The public becomes a mirror that magnifies everything, especially the parts of themselves that were never built to withstand that kind of scale. You see the effects of this every day on tour: the hypervigilance, the sudden withdrawals, the impulsive decisions, the impossibly thin skin in one moment and the impenetrable armor in the next. These are not signs of a "mentally ill artist." They are the predictable psychological consequences of being turned into an industry before you have finished becoming a person.

So when an artist tells you they do not need direction, they are not wrong. For most of their career, they truly haven't. The industry has not required self-examination from them. It has not asked them to think critically about their process. It has not challenged their instincts or demanded rigor or offered them a vocabulary for artistic growth. If anything, the industry has rewarded them most when they ignored advice, resisted guidance, or did the one thing that everyone around them insisted could never work. Their confidence is not arrogance. It is conditioning. It is the survival instinct of someone who learned early that their intuitive choices were the only stable currency in a world built to extract from them endlessly.

This is also why the idea of direction feels threatening. In their experience, the only people who have tried to "help" them have been people attempting to control them: labels pushing for a hit, managers pushing for a brand, producers pushing for a sound, choreographers pushing for a look. They have been shaped, molded, and managed so aggressively that the very concept of direction has fused in their mind with a loss of autonomy. What they resist is not you. What they resist is the memory of being treated as raw material. They fear becoming a passenger in their own show.

This means you cannot meet their resistance head-on. You cannot win an argument about expertise or hierarchy. You cannot persuade them with theory or reassure them with credentials. If you try, you will only confirm what they already believe—that direction is another form of control waiting to happen. Your job, instead, is to understand the world they are standing in, the emotional physics that govern their behavior, and the history that taught them to protect themselves from anyone who seems to be steering. Artists who say they don't need help are not announcing independence. They are announcing a wound.

This is where your work begins—not by challenging their confidence, but by entering their logic without threatening it. Direction in this context cannot start as authority; it has to start as translation. You have to understand their instincts before you can shape them, and you have to show them that direction is not a cage but a refinement of the impulses they already trust. The artist does not need to believe in directing as a concept. They only need to believe in you. And that belief is earned not by asserting your vision but by demonstrating, over and over again, that you are here to expand theirs rather than replace it.

In the next section, we'll talk about how to speak the artist's language—how to work inside their instinctive framework without diminishing it, and how to introduce the idea of direction as something that strengthens their autonomy instead of threatening it.

Speaking the Artist's Language

Before you can direct an artist who believes they do not need direction, you have to learn their language—not the language they use in interviews, and not the language of their public persona, but the deeper, more subterranean vocabulary that has shaped their work long before you arrived. This means immersing yourself fully in the world they have already created. Not casually. Not selectively. Obsessively. You study every album, every B-side, every alternate take, every performance that still floats around on the internet. You go through past interviews, not for gossip but for patterns: the phrases they repeat, the insecurities they return to, the subjects they avoid, the dreams they articulate without realizing it. You watch bootleg footage from tours they don't even remember. You scan old forums, fan discussions, archived social media accounts that haven't been touched in a decade. You gather everything they have ever offered the world, even the parts they pretended were accidental.

Ninety-nine percent of this research will never surface in the work you do together, and that is precisely the point. You are not collecting trivia. You are learning the emotional grammar of someone who has spent their life being observed but rarely understood. Every artist has a private logic—a set of internal rules that govern why certain choices make sense to them, even when they seem irrational to everyone else. If you don't understand that logic, you will speak the wrong language. You will offer ideas that sound elegant to you but land as noise to them. You will misunderstand their instincts because you have not yet learned the patterns beneath them. Artists who do not want direction are hypersensitive to misinterpretation; the moment you reveal that you don't understand their ecosystem, they retreat. But when they realize you have studied their world more thoroughly than anyone ever has—when you demonstrate knowledge of not just what they made but why they made it—you earn access that cannot be negotiated any other way.

Only after this immersion do you begin the real conversation. You set aside two days—never rushed, never transactional—and you ask every question that your research has generated. Not as an interrogation. As curiosity. As an attempt to understand the human architecture beneath the work. You ask about a lyric they wrote at 17, and whether they still stand by it. You ask why a certain chord progression appears across three albums. You ask about that amplifier they used on the early demos that never turned up again. You ask where they grew up, what the first album they bought was, what the first song they felt proud of was, what they were trying to prove, who they were trying to impress, what they were trying to escape. You ask the small questions because the small questions reveal the big truths. And you do something that almost no one in their life ever does: you don't write any of it down.

This is the difference. Managers take notes. Journalists take notes. A&R executives take notes. Therapists take notes. Everyone who has ever asked them questions has been documenting them, archiving them, turning their answers into data, strategy, or content. You are the first person who is not collecting anything. You are not building a file. You are building rapport. The absence of a notebook changes the temperature of the room. It signals that the conversation is not a transaction but an exploration. It communicates that you are listening for understanding, not for evidence. Over time, this unlocks a kind of honesty that cannot be forced. The artist begins to speak in a different register—less curated, less defensive, less rehearsed. They stop performing answers and start revealing them.

These interviews are not research; they are calibration. You are tuning your ear to their frequency. You are learning how they use language, how they remember themselves, how they interpret their own work. You are watching for the moments when their eyes light up, when their energy drops, when they move quickly past a subject that clearly matters. You are learning the artist not as the world sees them, but as they see themselves. And once you learn that, you can speak to them in a way that feels native—so native that the idea of direction stops feeling like an intrusion and starts feeling like a continuation of a conversation they have been having with themselves for years.

Building Trust and Earning Influence

Once you have immersed yourself in the artist's world—once you have studied every corner of their past work, listened to how they describe themselves, and spent real time with them without taking a single note—the relationship enters a different phase. You are no longer a stranger offering opinions. You are someone who speaks their language fluently enough for direction to happen without ever announcing itself as direction. And this is essential, because an artist who has spent their life protecting their instincts will not follow instructions, but they will follow interest.

The mistake most directors make in this situation is to begin with placement: "Stand here. Face this way. Move on this line." These are reasonable notes in a theater rehearsal, where the actors expect to be shaped by someone else and have the training to translate those instructions into emotional logic. Pop artists do not grow up in that culture. To them, a directional command is not a neutral request; it is a threat to the instinct that built their entire career. Even if the note is correct, even if it would dramatically strengthen the scene, the artist's body hears it as interference. It activates every defense they have learned to use against people who tried to control their image, their sound, or their identity.

So instead of directing in the traditional sense, you let the artist go through the scene as they naturally would. You watch them closely—not as a choreographer marking errors, but as an anthropologist documenting behavior. You observe the moment when they drift to the wrong sightline, or turn upstage, or abandon the picture you had planned. You let the moment happen. And then afterwards, in the quiet space that follows, you ask what might be the most important question in the entire process: "When you got to that mark, what made you turn the other way?"

This question is deceptively simple, but its effect is profound. You are not correcting them. You are not telling them they were wrong. You are inviting them to articulate their instinct. And because you have already built trust—because you spent two days learning the history beneath their gestures—they will tell you. They will explain what they were feeling, or what they were trying to emphasize, or what they were protecting themselves from. They will reveal the logic behind the choice, even if that logic is emotional, unconscious, or tangled.

Now you are not fighting their instinct. You are understanding it.

Once the instinct is on the table, once they see that you are genuinely interested in their reasoning rather than overriding it, you can begin to guide the moment toward something stronger. You don't say, "Do it this way." You say, "What would happen if we tried it with your energy pointed toward the audience instead of away from them?" or "If the moment is about withdrawal, what happens if we show the withdrawal with your face instead of your back?" You frame the adjustment in the language of their intention, not your command. The note becomes a conversation, not a correction.

And because the trust is real—because they know you have studied them with more rigor than anyone in their orbit—they are willing to experiment. Not because they want to obey you, but because they feel understood. For perhaps the first time in their career, direction feels like an extension of their own thinking rather than an interruption of it. The experiment becomes theirs. They try the moment another way. They discover that it feels truer, or more exposed, or more powerful. And as soon as they feel the improvement in their body, the note becomes embodied—no longer something you asked for, but something they arrived at themselves.

This is what influence looks like in the world of artists who claim they don't need help. It is not authority. It is alignment. It is the slow, patient construction of a shared language that allows you to shape the work from the inside rather than pressing on it from the outside. And once that dynamic is established, the artist stops resisting direction because direction stops feeling like direction. It feels like collaboration. It feels like protection. It feels like someone finally helping them make the version of the show they always imagined but never had the tools to construct alone.

This is the moment you have been working toward—not the moment when the artist follows your notes, but the moment when the artist invites them.

Chapter 20
The Case Studies
Great Concerts that Got It Right

How to Study a Concert: Annotated Examples

Studying a concert is not the same as remembering it. Memory clings to the spectacle—lights, volume, crowd, the moment you felt something. But those sensations do not help you direct. To learn from a concert, you must study it the way a watchmaker studies a clock: by examining the mechanisms that create the effect, not the effect itself. Fortunately, good video exists for most of the productions discussed in this chapter and can be found online. The exception is the *Life of Pablo* tour, which was so innovative that it became nearly impossible to record accurately; in that case, you will need to watch footage from multiple angles to understand how the world operated. Whenever possible, seek out video taken from a fixed audience position—the way the show was actually seen. And for *Welcome to My Nightmare*, there is a DVD release with a commentary track that is worth studying closely; it contains a wealth of practical insight into how the production was built.

What follows are annotated examples drawn from seven influential productions. Each one solves a particular problem with unusual clarity. Each one offers a system of decisions, not a string of highlights.

Alice Cooper—*Welcome to My Nightmare* (1975)

At first glance, the show appears revolutionary: a rock performance threaded with horror tableaux, choreographed violence, and theatrical

DOI: 10.4324/9781003679332-20

illusions. But the deeper truth is far more instructive. *Welcome to My Nightmare* is built almost entirely from vaudeville vocabulary—sight gags, grotesquerie, blackout illusions, and tightly timed stage business. It succeeds not because Cooper invented a new language, but because he revived an old one at a scale the form had never previously enjoyed.

The real innovation lies elsewhere: Cooper projected 35mm film upstage and forced the live cast to interact with it precisely. Every cue had a fixed duration. Every gesture had to land inside a pre-established cinematic rhythm. This is the opposite of improvisation; it is choreography against a metronome that never varies. In other words, the show only functions because the performers rehearse like dancers working with an unforgiving partner.

The lesson for directors is simple: the moment you introduce a rigid technical element—a film loop, a timed mechanical effect, a lighting chase—the human performance must become even more flexible, more controlled, and more disciplined. Technology that cannot bend requires actors and musicians who can.

Pink Floyd—*The Wall* (1980)

Some productions build a world; *The Wall* builds a barrier between the audience and the world. This distinction matters. The staging choices are not ornamental but architectural. As the wall grows, so does the emotional distance between performer and audience. The performers literally disappear behind their own construction. What looks like spectacle is, in fact, dramaturgy: alienation expressed through masonry.

The show succeeds because it treats scale as meaning, not as decoration. Every brick placed onstage alters the relationship between the audience and the performer. Every projection reinforces a thematic fracture. Most concerts chase immersion; *The Wall* deliberately denies it. That denial is what gives the eventual collapse its impact.

A director studying this show must look past the famous iconography and examine the structural logic: Who can see the performer at any given moment? How close do they appear? How does the set redraw the emotional map of the venue from minute to minute? Architecture is story.

U2—*Zoo TV* (1992)

Most commentary focuses on the visual overload—screens stacked on screens, newsfeeds, camera intrusions, saturated color, industrial noise, fragmentation. But the true meaning of *Zoo TV* lies in what it was reacting against. The previous tour had been built on sincerity, earnest musicianship, and emotional directness. The band rejected all of it. The show becomes legible only when understood as a staged act of reinvention.

Every design element reflects that rejection. The screens overwhelm the performer, the performer mocks his own mythology, and the production embraces contradiction rather than resolution. It is not chaos; it is choreography designed to break an earlier artistic identity into pieces.

For directors, the lesson is that a concert does not begin on opening night. It begins in the shadow of the last show. Audiences carry that memory with them, even if they never articulate it. Your staging choices are always part of a lineage—sometimes in alignment with the artist's history, sometimes in defiance of it. *Zoo TV* demonstrates what happens when an entire production is built on the act of turning away.

Madonna—*MDNA* (2012)

Whether audiences "liked" *MDNA* is irrelevant. The show was built with the precision of a cathedral—dense, meticulous, humorless in its commitment to its own aesthetic. What makes it extraordinary is not novelty but fluency. Almost every designer, choreographer, technician, and creative lead on this show had been working together since the late 1980s. They shared a common vocabulary forged over decades. The show is the apex of that shared language.

This also gives *MDNA* its strange finality. It marks the end of a specific era of arena and stadium touring—the last large-scale production created by a touring ecosystem that had evolved together over 25 years. Death, retirement, and industry change ensured that this configuration of collaborators would never assemble again.

Studying *MDNA* means studying integration. It is a reminder that some forms of coherence are only possible when teams work together over long spans of time. You cannot replicate the era, but you can study the results: a show in which every department speaks in the same dialect, without hesitation or compromise.

Kanye West—*The Life of Pablo* (*Saint Pablo Tour*) (2016)

This production redefines the concert not by building a world onstage but by suspending one above the audience. The floating platform is not an effect. It is the stage's governing metaphor. The performer becomes an object in orbit; the audience becomes the terrain. Light behaves like weather. Distance behaves like narrative.

What appears simple is actually the result of precise spatial engineering. The moving stage dictates the performer's blocking. The lights dictate the emotional temperature. The crowd responds as a single organism because they share the same visual field and the same gravitational center.

The critical takeaway is that spatial relationships are dramaturgical. If you move the performer vertically, the audience's emotional relationship to them transforms instantly. Intimacy, dominance, vulnerability, and scale all shift without a single lyric or gesture changing. The world is built not from scenery but from geometry.

Poppy—*Poppy.Computer Tour* (2017)

Where most concerts build a stable world, Poppy's staging builds instability. Identity breakdown is not a theme but a design principle. The visuals borrow from Internet aesthetics, performance art, horror imagery, and pop tropes, often in rapid succession. The performers behave as though the world is glitching—because dramaturgically, it is.

This is not randomness; it is commitment. Every costume change, lighting cue, and movement sequence supports the idea that the performer's identity is unstable, slippery, or manufactured. The audience is not asked to accept a single world. They are asked to accept that the world may rewrite itself at any moment.

The lesson here is that incoherence can be coherent—if it is intentional and rigorously executed. A concert does not need a singular identity to function; it needs a singular logic. Poppy's production offers one: the world is unstable, therefore the staging must be as well.

Air—*Air Play Moon Safari* (2024)

This production creates a world by ignoring all others. The set is a self-contained box—fixed dimensions, fixed proportions, fixed atmosphere. It does not respond to the architecture of the venue. It does not acknowledge the crowd. It is a sealed environment carried from city to city like a museum installation.

Because of this rigidity, compromises follow. Stage space tightens. Performer movement narrows. Audience engagement shifts from interaction to observation. But this purity is the point. The world is complete only when untouched by external context.

What the production proves is that consistency can be more powerful than adaptation. While many touring shows attempt to "fill" the venue, *Moon Safari (Live)* refuses to. It establishes a visual identity so strong that the surrounding space becomes irrelevant. For directors, the principle is simple: sometimes the correct solution is not to scale your world but to protect it.

What Worked and Why: Patterns Across Seven Shows

When you place these concerts beside one another—not as cultural artifacts but as pieces of staged craft—a set of shared principles begins to appear. Although the aesthetics differ wildly, the underlying mechanics are remarkably consistent. Each production builds a world with clarity, places the performers within that world with intention, and makes choices that reinforce the logic of that world no matter how inconvenient or counterintuitive those choices may be. What follows is not a list of techniques but an attempt to articulate the structural forces that make these concerts hold together when so many others drift into incoherence.

The first pattern is the primacy of worldbuilding. In every example, the world comes before the effects. *Welcome to My Nightmare* begins with vaudeville logic, not shock value; the horror elements only work because they belong to a theatrical language more than a century old. *The Wall* constructs its world through architecture, brick by brick, turning stagecraft into a psychological landscape. *Zoo TV* builds a world of media saturation and fragmentation, not because screens were fashionable, but because the band needed a vocabulary that contradicted their previous earnestness. *MDNA* constructs a world out of decades of shared practice. Kanye's *Saint Pablo* invents a world suspended above the audience. Poppy creates a world that is unstable by design. Air builds a sealed environment that ignores the venue entirely. None of these worlds emerge accidentally. Each one dictates the staging rather than being reverse-engineered from it.

Weak productions gather ideas first and attempt to discover a world afterward. Strong productions choose a world and allow the decisions to fall into place around it.

A second pattern emerges from the way these shows handle distance—the physical and emotional relationship between performer and audience. Distance is never coincidental. In *The Wall*, the distance grows until the performers vanish behind their own construction, turning alienation into architecture. In *Saint Pablo*, the performer's elevation creates a new kind of intimacy, one in which thousands of people share a single vantage point beneath a moving gravitational center. Air's rigid box keeps the performers at a measured remove regardless of venue size, shifting the relationship from participation to observation. Even in less extreme examples, the distance is calibrated deliberately: Cooper uses proximity for theatrical immediacy; Madonna uses scale to produce a kind of ritualized spectacle; U2 and Poppy constantly renegotiate their distance through screens, choreography, and identity shifts. Directors who ignore distance allow the venue to choose it for them.

Scale, too, only succeeds when it has meaning. The wall in *The Wall* is not a backdrop—it is the plot. The deluge of screens in *Zoo TV* is not decoration—it is the antagonist. The vast machinery of *MDNA* reflects fluency, not vanity; it is the result of collaborators who have spent decades refining a shared aesthetic grammar. By contrast, *Air* demonstrates how refusing to scale can be equally expressive: by carrying a fixed world from venue to venue, the band asserts that consistency matters more than filling available space. Scale becomes powerful only when it tells the audience something about the world they are entering.

Technology functions in a similar way. These shows reveal that technology is never neutral. It alters timing, rhythm, and behavior. In Cooper's production, the 35mm film loops create an unyielding tempo that the performers must learn to navigate. In *Zoo TV*, the cameras do not merely record; they destabilize the performer's presence by reframing it constantly. The floating platform of *Saint Pablo* becomes a physical partner to the performer, dictating gesture, breath, and stillness. Madonna's automated elements only work because every cue is woven into her physical timing. Even Poppy's glitch aesthetics require absolute human commitment to each abrupt transformation. Air's sealed world forces the performers into a minimal, controlled vocabulary. In every case, the technology shapes the human performance, not the other way around.

Another shared principle is reinvention through rejection. Some of these concerts only make sense in the context of what they refuse to continue. *Zoo TV* is a direct repudiation of U2's previous sincerity; without that context, the show reads merely as sensory overload instead of intentional self-disruption. Poppy's work rejects the stable pop persona. Kanye's floating stage rejects the traditional proscenium. Reinvention is not an accessory—it is dramaturgy. Directors must understand the show not only as a standalone object but as part of the artist's ongoing narrative.

Consistency emerges through two contrasting pathways. Some productions achieve it through fluency, as in *MDNA*, where long-term collaborators share instincts so deeply that the show feels authored by a single mind. Others achieve it through purity, as in Air's *Moon Safari (Live)*, where the production maintains coherence by refusing to acknowledge the external world. These methods appear opposed, yet they produce a similar effect: an atmosphere in which every choice belongs to the same universe. What they reveal is that coherence must be either inherited or enforced—never assumed.

Perhaps the most important pattern is that innovation rarely comes from novelty. Instead, it comes from recombining existing tools under new pressure. Cooper revives vaudeville. Floyd turns set construction into narrative. U2 uses broadcast media grammar onstage. Madonna crystallizes decades of collaborational evolution. Kanye repurposes industrial rigging into dramaturgy. Poppy merges Internet logic with live performance. Air applies installation-art principles to touring. None of these solutions appear out of nowhere; they are old tools arranged with new intention.

Finally, all of these shows share one essential characteristic: they obey their own internal logic, even when doing so risks alienating the audience. *MDNA* remains severe in its commitment to its world. *Zoo TV* refuses to clarify itself. *The Wall* accepts its own emotional distance.

Saint Pablo adheres to its vertical logic without offering conventional staging as compensation. Poppy's instability never resolves. Air never adapts its world to the venue. Coherence requires commitment, not popularity. A show collapses the moment its creators begin to second-guess the rules of the world they have made.

Understanding these patterns will allow you to apply their underlying principles rather than their surface aesthetics.

Applying the Lessons: Building Your Own Show

It is easy, when you admire a production, to mistake replication for authorship. Popular music has already offered a clear example of this trap. Much of Marilyn Manson's stage vocabulary—its shock devices, its grotesque humor, its ritualized violence—comes directly from Alice Cooper's work, often replicated so literally that anyone familiar with Cooper's shows can map the lineage beat for beat. For younger audiences, the borrowing may pass unnoticed, but that does not give it artistic value. A copied world is never a coherent world; it is a costume worn over someone else's ideas. Imitation can sustain a career, but it cannot direct a show.

Every example in this chapter offers a reminder that a directed concert must arise from the internal rules of its own world. That world should be particular to the artist you are working with, the moment they are standing in, and the story they need to tell right now. If you build a world by borrowing someone else's choices, you inherit their problems, not their solutions.

Treat these case studies as stepping stones, not blueprints. They show you what is possible when a director commits completely to a world—any world—and refuses to weaken it. They show you how craft evolves, how ideas sharpen over decades, and how one strong decision can define an entire production. Your task is to move the craft forward, not to replicate its past victories. The future of concert direction will not come from repeating what worked before, but from applying the same rigor, courage, and clarity to ideas that belong only to your show.

Chapter 21
Directing Your First Show

What to Expect

Directing your first show is an initiation, and like all initiations, it comes with a strange asymmetry of responsibility. You will discover very quickly that the director is the person everyone looks to when something goes wrong, and the last person anyone thinks of when something goes right. The lighting board fails halfway through a cue run. It will somehow be your fault. A performer forgets a line, a tech gets the time wrong, a scenic element arrives damaged, a volunteer misreads an email—these belong to you now. Not because you caused them, but because directing is the job of inheriting every problem whether or not you touched the mechanism that created it. You are the person who holds the shape of the show, which means you also hold every fracture.

What no one warns you about is the reverse: the victories, the moments of clarity, the cues that land so cleanly they feel inevitable—those rarely belong to you in the room. When something works beautifully, the performer feels they found it. The designer feels their inspiration finally landed. The tech team feels they solved a puzzle you didn't even see. And they are all right. Everyone's contribution did make that moment. Your contribution, however, will be invisible because the best directing often is. If the world you built is functioning, no one notices the person who built it.

You must understand this imbalance early, or it will eat at you. New directors sometimes flinch when the blame comes their way and bristle when the praise goes elsewhere. They mistake both for commentary

DOI: 10.4324/9781003679332-21

on their worth. They look for recognition, or fairness, or proof that they are doing the job correctly. But directing is not a job that rewards you with applause, or even acknowledgment. It rewards you with the show itself—with the knowledge that the work is coherent, precise, alive. That must be enough.

The temptation, especially in a first production, is to internalize every complaint and amplify every compliment. Do neither. The blame is almost never as personal as it sounds. The praise is almost never as complete as it feels. Both are static. Both distort your understanding of the work. Your task is to keep your attention on the thing you are building, not on how the room interprets your role in building it. The room will always interpret you through the lens of its own needs: some will want you to be a parent, others a therapist, others a boss, others a shield. If you try to satisfy every projection, you will stop doing the job.

The truth is simple and unsentimental: expect to be misunderstood. Expect to be held responsible for problems you didn't create. Expect to receive little credit for the problems you solved before anyone else even knew they existed. And then—expect none of it to matter. Your first show is where you learn the central discipline of directing: the discipline of attention. Keep yours on the work. Let the noise pass through you like weather. The show does not care about credit or blame. It only cares whether it breathes.

Practical Checklist

The practical reality of directing your first show is that you must become more organized than you think any human being reasonably should be. Not tidy—organized. Tidy is aesthetic. Organized is survival. Touring, producing, or even mounting a single extended run will eventually strip you down to whatever systems you built before exhaustion set in, and if those systems are flimsy or improvised, you will discover that fact at the worst possible moment, usually in a loading dock at 3am. with no wifi. So begin with this assumption: in future you will be sleep-deprived, overextended, emotionally threadbare, and asked a question that must be answered immediately. Build for that person, not the optimistic version of yourself who is currently well-rested and hydrated.

Before you even start rehearsals, spend a full month making your checklist. Not a weekend. Not an afternoon. A month. Keep the document open—physically or mentally—at all times. You will remember things in the middle of the day, in the shower, during another meeting, halfway through a meal. You will discover needs you didn't know existed: a page-by-page cue reference sheet, a master troubleshooting log (so you can remember how you solved a problem the last time it occurred), a diagram of the stage clocking exact spike-mark distances, cough drops, a blue and black Sharpie, and whatever else makes sense in your situation. Every day adds a new layer. Every week reveals a blind spot you hadn't considered. By the end of 30 days you will not have a perfect list, but you will have something dense enough, specific enough, and honest enough to build from. The checklist becomes the seed of the systems you create—your map of the world before you have set foot in it. When you leave home, this checklist should be at the top of the bag that you take with you.

I stated this earlier in this book, but I must reiterate it: this means keeping two complete sets of records for everything—notes, plots, versions of cues, contact lists, schedules, diagrams, budgets, set dimensions, lighting states, prop inventories, wardrobe needs, and every eccentric scrap of information that keeps a show alive. You will not know which piece you need until the moment you need it, and by then it will be too late to go searching. One system should live digitally—organized in folders, labeled with actual words instead of emotional guesses, synced across devices, accessible even when your laptop dies. The other must be on paper, printed cleanly, stored in a binder you could hand to a stranger who would instantly understand the world of the show. Because at some point a battery will fail, a drive will corrupt, a cloud service will go down, or someone will spill coffee on your only laptop 15 minutes before soundcheck.

Backups are not paranoia; they are infrastructure. Have backups for your backups, not because you expect catastrophe but because catastrophe is the baseline condition of touring work. You will spend months in transit—vans, buses, planes, green rooms, anonymous hotel hallways, repurposed storage closets masquerading as dressing rooms. Your belongings will be shuffled, repacked, borrowed, misplaced. Your brain will operate at half capacity but be expected to output full authority. The only stable elements will be the systems you designed before the chaos began.

Think of yourself as a turtle. Your entire environment travels with you, wrapped around your body, a shell filled with the maps, tools, and fragments of the world you are responsible for maintaining. You cannot control the terrain, the weather, the predators, the detours, or the endless list of small disasters. But you can control what you carry, and you can control how quickly you can reach into your shell and pull out exactly what the moment requires. That is the function of the practical checklist—not a list of tasks, but a portable world you can live inside when the external one dissolves.

If you design your systems well, you won't need to think. And for long stretches of a tour, that is the highest luxury: not efficiency, not elegance, but the ability to act without hesitation because the groundwork was done before the storm arrived. Your systems are the version of you that will keep the show standing when your body and brain cannot.

Mental and Emotional Preparation

The final preparation you make—the one no one sees and no one can do for you—is the internal one. Directing your first show will change the way you experience pressure, conflict, exhaustion, and praise. It will pull at every loose thread in your personality. It will confront you with the parts of yourself you thought you had outgrown and the parts you didn't know were fragile. You cannot prepare for all of it, but you can prepare for the impact.

The first thing to understand is that your emotional metabolism is now part of the room. The cast and crew will read your face before they read the schedule. They will feel your tension before you speak. They will interpret your silence as fear, your efficiency as coldness, your enthusiasm as favoritism, your fatigue as disappointment. None of these interpretations will be accurate, but they will shape the environment. This means you must develop a calm center—not saintly, not detached, just steady. You need a place inside yourself that does not wobble when something goes wrong, because things will go wrong constantly. Your steadiness becomes the room's steadiness.

You also need to accept that directing is an emotional asymmetry: you will give more than you receive. You will spend weeks pouring clarity, encouragement, and focus into others, and very little of that will flow back to you. The show will ask you to be patient when no one else is being patient, to be generous when no one else is being generous, to be the adult when everyone else is busy being an artist. This is not unfair; it is the job. The sooner you stop expecting reciprocity, the sooner you free yourself to work without resentment.

Exhaustion will warp your sense of scale. Small problems will feel enormous. Innocent questions will feel accusatory. A flawed run will feel like the collapse of the entire production. You have to train yourself to see the difference between reality and fatigue. Fatigue will lie to you. It will tell you the show is falling apart, that the cast doesn't trust you, that you've made a mistake in taking this on. When that voice appears—and it will—you must treat it as weather. It will pass. The work is almost always stronger than your panic.

There will also be the opposite trap: the emotional high. The night a run finally clicks, the moment a performer breaks through, the rehearsal where everything feels alive—you will want to believe the show is fixed, that your instincts are flawless, that the hard part is behind you. This, too, is weather. Momentum is precious, but it is not permanence. Do not get drunk on breakthrough days; they are bursts of oxygen, not proof of invincibility.

The deeper emotional preparation is understanding that directing is not about control—it is about containment. You are not shaping perfect conditions; you are shaping a space where imperfection can still function. The cast will have off days. The crew will make mistakes. Venues will sabotage your best-laid plans. You will feel your grasp loosen. And yet the world of the show must hold. Your job is not to eliminate chaos but to build a structure that can absorb it without breaking.

Finally, you must make peace with solitude. Directing is collaborative in the room and lonely everywhere else. After rehearsals, while the cast unwinds and the crew decompresses, you will sit with the questions no one else can answer: What is the show missing? What did the run reveal? What needs to change tomorrow? This solitude is not a punishment; it is where clarity forms. Learn to sit with it without resenting it. Learn to trust the silence that follows a long day. Often the best directing happens there—when the noise of the room falls away and the internal compass resets.

If you can cultivate steadiness, generosity, perspective, containment, and solitude, you will enter your first production with something sturdier than confidence. You will enter with resilience—the thing that will carry you through the days when nothing works, the days when everything works, and all the days in between.

Chapter 22
Final Thoughts
Why This Matters

The Director as Silent Architect

By now you've noticed the cruel paradox at the center of this job: the better you are at it, the less anyone will ever see you. When a concert works—really works—the audience does not walk out saying, "The architecture was coherent," or "The internal logic held," or "Every cue obeyed the world's emotional physics." They walk out saying, "That was amazing," and then they attribute that amazement to the only person whose name they know. Which is how it should be. The artist should get the credit. The artist should shine. You built the frame for their light, not the light itself.

But that invisibility leaves a question hanging in the air, one you have to answer honestly if you're going to last:

> If the audience can't see your work, and most of the industry doesn't understand it, and the only time your name gets mentioned is when something goes wrong—why do this at all?

Because somewhere inside you there is a person who cares about the integrity of the world, even when the world is temporary.

Because someone has to care about the shape of the evening when no one else is even thinking in shapes.

Because concerts—left to habit, convenience, and commerce—will always collapse toward entropy unless someone is quietly, relentlessly giving them form.

The director is that someone.

DOI: 10.4324/9781003679332-22

You are the silent architect of an art form that rarely acknowledges it even has architecture. You are the person who holds the blueprint while everyone else is holding a cable, an instrument, a checklist, a costume, a cue stack, or a fear. You are the one thinking about coherence while the industry thinks about gross potential. You are the one thinking about emotional arc while the audience thinks about hearing their favorite song. You are the one thinking about the show as a complete organism while everyone else interacts with it as a task, a problem, or a thrill.

And that is the point.

If you wanted applause, you would have chosen another job. If you wanted your name on a billboard, you would have chosen another medium. Direction is not a spotlight profession; it is a gravitational one. Your work pulls every scattered idea, every competing department, every impulsive artistic instinct into alignment so that the show can stand upright on its own legs. You are the force that makes meaning possible, not the face that gets thanked for it.

The work requires an almost unreasonable level of devotion. You will sweat details the audience will never notice. You will protect moments they forget five minutes later. You will build systems that only reveal their necessity when they fail. You will watch decisions age in real time—some beautifully, some embarrassingly—and you will still get up the next morning to do it again.

Why?

Because someone has to care about more than the night.

Someone has to care about the medium.

If concerts are ever going to evolve beyond the cultural assumption that they are merely loud gatherings, product showcases, or nostalgia engines—if they are ever going to stand shoulder-to-shoulder with theater and opera in artistic legitimacy—then intention has to live somewhere. And it lives in you. Quietly. Patiently. Without applause. Without fanfare. Without certainty that anyone will notice.

You are the architect of something that moves through people's bodies long before it reaches their minds. You are the custodian of focus in a world addicted to distraction. You are the one who ensures that a concert is not just "working," but alive. And even if no one sees the architecture you built, everyone will feel the stability it creates.

This is why the job matters.

This is why you do it.

Because without someone designing the invisible, the visible falls apart.

A Call for Better Shows

If you look long enough at the touring industry, you begin to see how much of it is held together by habits that no one remembers choosing. A show succeeds, another copies it, a third iteration becomes "standard practice," and eventually an entire art form starts mistaking repetition for inevitability. Most concerts are built from inherited assumptions that feel natural simply because they are familiar, and because familiarity is cheaper, faster, and easier to scale. The result is a medium that appears functional on the surface—tickets sell, crowds scream, trucks load out on time—but rarely pauses to examine whether "functional" is the same as "alive."

This is the central problem: concerts have quietly flattened into something strangely disposable. People talk about their night out, about how loud it was, about how close they stood to the stage, about what they posted online after. But they rarely talk about the show as a constructed experience. In many cases they can't, because the show wasn't constructed. It was assembled. The audience wasn't guided; they were serviced. They weren't brought somewhere new; they were escorted through a sequence of moments designed to be recognizable rather than meaningful.

It is tempting to blame the audience for this, to assume their expectations are limited or unsophisticated. But the truth is more uncomfortable: audiences can only respond to the possibilities they are offered. If every tour recycles the same emotional beats, the same pacing structures, the same aesthetic clichés, the same unexamined logic, then it is no surprise when even the most enthusiastic fans eventually stop caring. They were not disappointed by concerts. They were disappointed by lack of imagination.

Meanwhile, artists are aging in ways the medium still refuses to acknowledge. Many are making the most interesting work of their lives at 40, 50, 60. Their writing deepens, their point of view sharpens, their relationship to performance matures. But when they walk onstage, they often find themselves surrounded by the same staging vocabulary that was built for them 20 years earlier, as though time passed for the artist but not for the architecture surrounding them. The touring ecosystem continues to treat concerts as a youth-driven product, even as the people who make them and the people who attend them move deeper into their own history.

This stagnation is not the result of malicious intent. It is the inevitable outcome of a system where every department is incentivized to minimize risk. Managers are wary of anything that complicates marketing. Promoters need predictability. Sponsors require visibility. Agents want repeatable routing. Labels want brand alignment. And the artist—the one person with the most to gain from innovation—is often the one with the least time, the most pressure, and the largest machine around them urging caution. When a safe show sells out, everyone feels validated, even if the show itself was built from compromises rather than ideas.

But the consequences accumulate. People stop attending concerts not because they lose interest in live art, but because they have been taught that the medium will not surprise them. They assume they have already seen what there is to see. They believe the form has a ceiling. And once the audience believes the ceiling is low, the industry begins designing for that ceiling, which lowers it further, until the entire art form exists in a perpetual adolescence—loud, chaotic, energetic, but seldom purposeful.

This is why better shows matter. Not out of snobbery, not out of idealism, but out of responsibility. If a concert is going to summon an army of trucks, consume enormous resources, travel thousands of miles, occupy entire arenas, and leave behind a measurable environmental wake, then the work itself must justify the footprint. A show has to offer something more than recycled spectacle. Otherwise it becomes nothing more than noise—expensive, exhausting, creatively vacant noise.

Concerts once carried the weight of cultural transformation. They challenged authority, reshaped identity, shifted public imagination. They were not background entertainment; they were catalysts. If the medium feels diminished now, it is because too many shows have settled into the safety of familiarity. Progress requires friction. Renewal requires displacement. An art form cannot grow if it keeps choosing comfort over clarity.

This is where the director enters—not as a visionary imposing revolution, but as the person willing to ask the questions no one else has time to ask. What is the show trying to say? Why is this moment here? What is the emotional logic behind this transition? What is the world we are building, and what rules govern it? These questions are not luxuries. They are the pressure valves that keep the medium from drifting into irrelevance.

A better show does not require more money. It requires more intention. It asks you to push past the automatic habits of the industry and make choices that are specific, deliberate, and alive. And in a landscape where neither the audience nor the infrastructure knows how to demand that level of rigor, the responsibility falls to the one person who sees the whole shape of the evening: the director. If the medium is going to move forward, someone has to lead, even if no one notices the leading.

Which means the work falls to you. Not to win applause. Not to gain recognition. But to make the form worthy of itself.

Leaving a Legacy of Intention

The strange thing about directing concerts is that the work evaporates the moment it succeeds. A show that runs smoothly feels inevitable; a show that feels inevitable begins to seem simple; and once something feels simple, people assume no one really built it. This is the final trick of the medium: the more intentional you are, the more invisible you become. A directed show leaves no fingerprints. It stands on its own, balanced, coherent, alive—without revealing the labor that made it so.

And yet, the work endures, just not in the places anyone expects.

Every show you build joins a quiet lineage. Not the lineage of box-office numbers or tour grosses or backstage gossip, but the lineage of people who will someday watch a shaky cellphone video of your work long after the trucks have gone home. Time flattens trends. It erases hype. It strips away the context that once excused sloppy choices or masked incoherence. What remains is the structure: the clarity of the world, the logic of the staging, the intention behind the movement.

When you watch a concert from 10 or 15 years ago and it still feels alive, it is because someone cared at a level the audience never saw. Someone built a spine strong enough to stand without explanation.

This is the real legacy of direction—not the credit, not the thanks, not even the memory of the night—but the durability of the choices. A directed show ages differently. It carries itself. It holds its shape. It reveals its architecture slowly, sometimes long after its moment has passed. And that is why the work matters, even when the room does not understand it, even when the artist is too overwhelmed to articulate it, even when the audience is too exhilarated to notice it.

But the legacy you leave is not just the shows themselves. It is the standards you set in the rooms you lead. Every time you insist on coherence instead of convenience, you normalize intention. Every time you refuse to let a moment slide simply because "no one will notice," you teach the people around you that noticing is the job. Every time you articulate why something matters—even when you are the only one who sees it—you widen the vocabulary of what a concert can be for everyone who touches it.

People absorb these expectations silently. Crew members begin thinking dramaturgically. Artists begin thinking architecturally. Designers begin thinking narratively. Even if no one names these shifts, they accumulate. They carry forward. The next tour is a little sharper because you bothered to care on this one. The next associate has better instincts because they watched you build this system. The next artist asks deeper questions because you created a world where deeper questions had value.

This is how the medium evolves: through the steady, patient cultivation of intention.

And if that sounds small, remember how fragile this art form is. Concerts disappear the moment they end. They leave no physical residue. They exist only in the nervous system of the people who experienced them. That impermanence is not a flaw; it is the point. Live performance is the art of the vanishing moment. But intention gives the moment weight. It gives it density. It gives it an afterlife in the minds and bodies of the audience, even if they cannot articulate why.

Your work is the difference between a concert that evaporates the second the lights come up and a concert that lingers. Between a show that feels like noise and a show that feels like meaning. Between an evening people remember because they were close to the artist and an evening they remember because something inside them changed.

Most people will never know the role you played in that shift. They will thank the singer, the band, the lights, the costumes. They will use words like "vibe" and "energy" because they do not have another vocabulary. That is fine. They do not need one. If you have done your job well, they felt something. That is enough.

You do this work because you believe concerts can be more than their habits. You do it because the medium deserves a future that is smarter than its past. You do it because someone has to choose intention in a landscape that rarely rewards it. And you do it knowing that real change is slow, incremental, often invisible—but cumulative.

This book has given you the tools. It has warned you about the obstacles. It has shown you the realities of blame, the absence of credit, the distortions of exhaustion, and the fragility of coherence on the road. None of that is meant to discourage you. It is meant to prepare you. Because the truth is simple: directing concerts is difficult work in an industry that often misunderstands its own needs. But it is also necessary work, meaningful work, work that moves the medium forward one show at a time.

Your legacy will not be your name.

Your legacy will be the intention you put into the world.

And if you do this job well—quietly, patiently, stubbornly—then long after you leave the room, long after the tour ends, long after the footage is uploaded and forgotten and rediscovered by someone who wasn't there, the work will still hold. It will still speak. It will still matter.

That is the real reward. That is the reason to do the job. That is the legacy you leave when you choose intention over everything else.

Index

For Product Safety Concerns and Information please contact our EU representative GPSR@taylorandfrancis.com
Taylor & Francis Verlag GmbH, Kaufingerstraße 24, 80331 München, Germany

www.ingramcontent.com/pod-product-compliance
Lightning Source LLC
LaVergne TN
LVHW011155030926
847199LV00028B/303

* 9 7 8 1 0 4 1 1 5 4 1 7 4 *